agape
NOKIA
SAUCONY
ciol
Dynamics3
LAMIN-ART
The Art of Laminates
online
Lunesta
Jeep
DUNLOP
Husqvarna
SLK
Panasonic
PIRELLI
Teknion

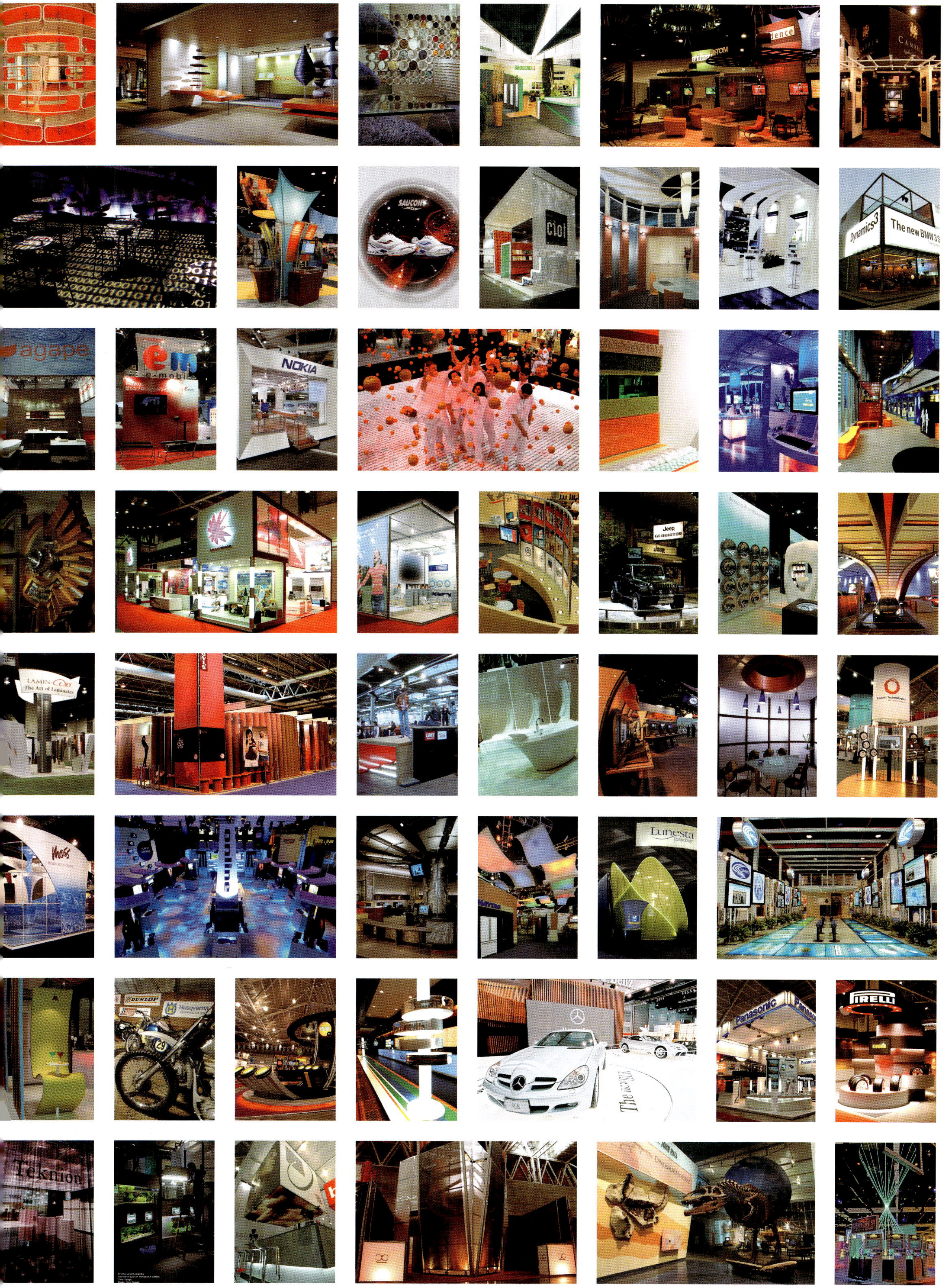

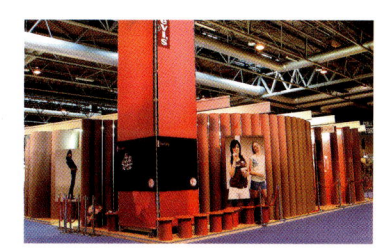

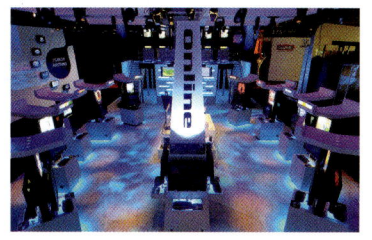

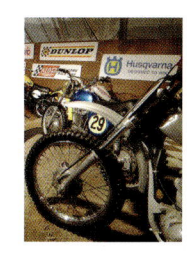

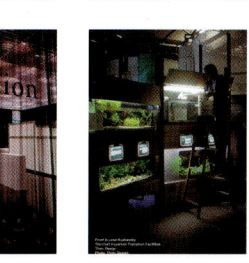

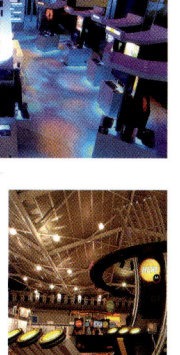

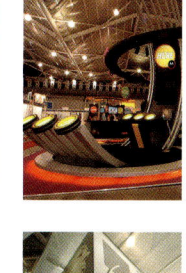

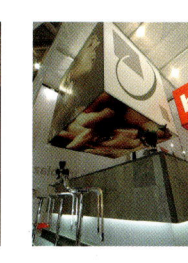

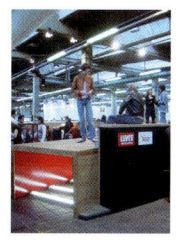

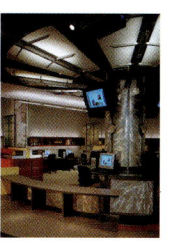

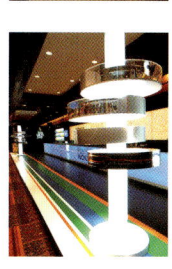

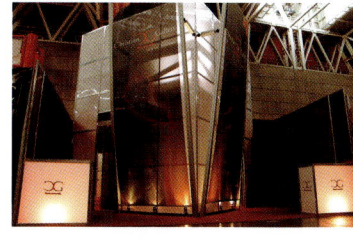

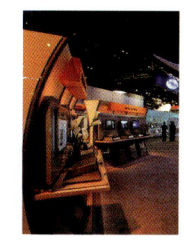

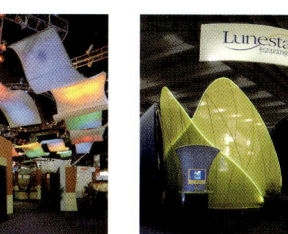

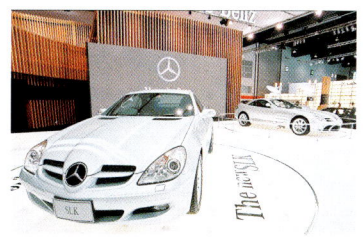

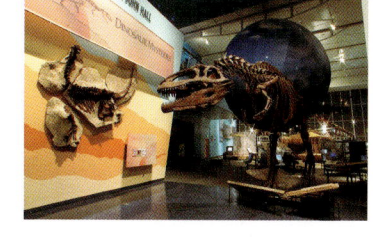

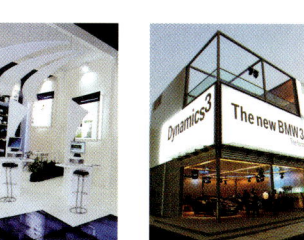

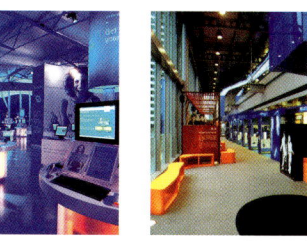

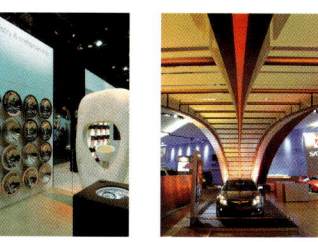

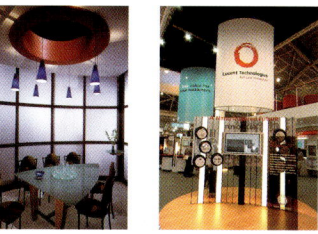

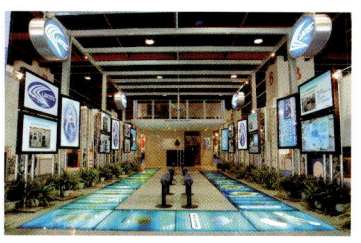

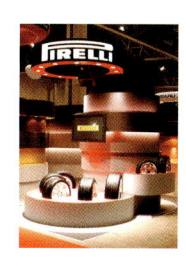

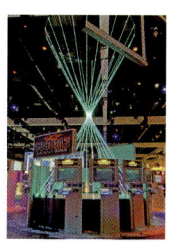

CONTEMPORARY
EXHIBIT DESIGN
No.2

MARTIN M. PEGLER

VISUAL REFERENCE PUBLICATIONS, INC. — NEW YORK

Visual Reference Publications, Inc.
302 Fifth Avenue
New York, NY 10001

Distributors to the trade in the United States and Canada
Watson-Guptill
770 Broadway
New York, NY 10003

Distributors outside the United States and Canada
HarperCollins International
10 East 53rd Street
New York, NY 10022-5299

Library of Congress Cataloging in Publication Data:
Contemporary Exhibit Design No. 2

Printed in China

The book is exclusively distributed in China
by Beijing Designerbooks Co., Ltd.
Building No.2, No.3, Babukou, Gulouxidajie,
Xicheng District, Beijing 100009, P.R.China
Tel: 0086(010)6406-7653 Fax: 0086(010)6406-0931
E-mail: info@designerbooks.net
http://www.designerbooks.net

ISBN: 1-58471-103-5

Book Design: Veronika Cherepanina

CONTENTS:

INTRODUCTION

Trade shows are an international phenomenon. The need for organizations, industries, manufacturers and retailers to get together to see what's new, who is doing what, and what will be the next big "thing" crosses all national boundaries. This phenomenon was, in the past, dominated by fairs and trade shows in the U.S. and Western Europe.

However, as third world countries are developing into second world countries and with middle classes growing in areas where they previously barely existed, retailers and manufacturers and all forms of communication technology are becoming vital threads in the retail fabric of those countries.

In this edition of Contemporary Exhibit Design we travel across the globe to look in on who is doing what and where. We are finding international campaigns being reinterpreted and redesigned—exhibit and trade show-wise—to suit the cultures they are being presented to. Exhibit designers trade shows are no longer just flourishing in the U.S. and the developed countries of Europe, but we are finding exhibit design talents and products of those talents all over the world. In this issue we travel across the U.S. to England, Germany and Russia— then on into Asia— the Arab Emirate of Qatar, Thailand, South Korea, China, Taiwan and over to Japan. We can see examples, as well, from New Zealand, Mexico and Brazil.

However, no matter where the trade show travels—and many are designed to travel—the basic requirements for a good exhibit are the same. Exhibits need to be easy to ship, easy to assemble and then to disassemble. The designs are often required to adapt to new and different spaces in different expo halls. Thus, many designers start with basic modular systems and concepts that accommodate to expansion or contraction—as needed. No matter where we look there is also a proliferation of variations on tension stretched fabric over aluminum frames as a technique for part, or all, of a trade show design. This technique permits big, sweeping and attention getting forms and partitions with little weight but lots of show and pizzazz.

Graphics and lighting are two vital components of all trade show designs and exhibits. If the stand is of any value it must first and foremost bring attention to the space. That means "attraction" and color and light attracts! High flying forms, totems and towers may be visible from across the expo hall but they need light—and color—to attract and draw visitors. Trade show floors are usually over-whelmed by conflicting colors and messages so it becomes essential to

Left:
PLAYSTATION

E3 2005, Los Angeles, CA
Design: *Mauk Design, San Francisco, CA*
Fabrication: *Pinnacle Exhibits*
Photography: *Andy Caulfield*

visually separate one space from its neighbors. In this edition the reader will often be able to read, in the designers' own words, what they did and with what to "separate" their space and to focus the attendees attention on the purpose of the booth. Once the attendee is brought into the space, graphics take over to "present" or "sell" the company's brand and its message. The reader will be able to see how the company's name, logo and signature colors are used in the design concept to further the brand image.

Entertainment is alive and demanding to be part of the exhibit design concept. People today everywhere are surrounded by sources of entertainment and so they have come to expect it at trade shows, in corporate headquarters, or even in museums. So—interactive stations, demo platforms, giant plasma screens, mini-theaters and presentation areas plus "hospitality" zones are being fitted into the booth along with products, samples and service explanations. Sometimes removed and sometimes a focal element in the total space are the one-on-one or group conferencing areas. This is where the business of the trade show is actually transacted. Often these areas are made to look "residential" to encourage the "buyers" to relax and be more at ease—and thus more responsive to the sales pitch.

We have also included a section on exhibits that appear in museums and corporate offices/headquarters where the main thrust is not to "sell" a product but to provide information, knowledge or background material that will eventually lead to—in some cases—a better brand acceptance on the part of the visitor. We have selected some museum type installations and some corporate office exhibits as well as some "good will" examples by company's taking advantage of some moment in time or some local event.

As the reader travels through "space"—and these projects are set out by the amount of space they cover—from a minimal 10 ft. by 20 ft. space to one that spreads out over tens of thousands of square feet—it is almost unimportant what language the exhibit "speaks." Whether it is in Las Vegas or London—in Sao Paulo, Shenzhen or Singapore, an exhibit is an exhibit and it is mainly designed to promote the brand, the logo and the product or service. We have selected almost 70 exhibits to prove that point. Enjoy the trip.

Martin M. Pegler

Right:
PLAYSTATION

E3 2005, Los Angeles, CA
Design: *Mauk Design, San Francisco, CA*
Fabrication: *Pinnacle Exhibits*
Photography: *Andy Caulfield*

CIOT MARBLE & TILE

Interior Design Show 2004, Toronto, ON
Design: *ll BY lV Design, Toronto, ON*
Photography: *David Whittaker*

How do you top the top? That was the problem facing CIOT Marble & Tile and their exhibit designers, II BY IV Design of Toronto. Year after year the booths designed for CIOT by II BY IV have won top awards at the Interior Design shows. For the new show the designers were faced with creating "a dramatic way to demonstrate the versatility of CIOT's products and to inspire innovative thinking among architects and interior designers." What they came up with and is shown here is "hip, colorful and curvaceous."

At opposite ends of a plain white rectangular suspended ceiling panel glittering expanses of metallic "daisy chains" were hung that incorporated giant logos. Within, on a simple platform in shiny white tile edged in stainless steel, II BY IV placed a single huge continuous bent form made of MD, and here they delineated several types of living/working spaces including a meeting place and a presentation theater—all within 250 sq. ft.

To introduce CIOT's product range, each face of the structure was surfaced with a new and exciting mosaic tile that reflected the glow of the discreet, down and up lighting of the booth. The tile colors ranged from lime green to tomato red and the tiles were selected from the new Glass Three lines that included: Iridium, Murano and Waterford tiles. To complete the display there were decorative touches such as a sleek, wall-mounted faucet

above an art glass basin, plump round pillows covered in persimmon fabric, wall mounted display shelves, storage units in matching high gloss finish and a vertical slab of mirror.

"Show visitors were astounded by the versatility, adaptability and creative opportunity afforded by these stunning new materials and the deceptively uncomplicated display that demonstrated them."

DESIGN COMPENDIUM

**A&B Store Expo 2004, New York,
    NY & ICFF 2005, New York, NY**
Design: *Design Compendium, New York, NY*
Photography: *Courtesy of Design Compendium*

The modular exhibit was designed by Design Compendium to introduce this design firm's many talents and services. The booth design was originally introduced in a 200 sq. ft. space and later expanded to fit the 300 sq. ft. space at the ICFF show in 2005.

The back wall was treated with 42 stripes that ranged in width from 2 in. to 12 in. and they were all 47 in. tall. "Each stripe was made from a material that had been used for various projects created by us–as well as some materials we would like to have the opportunity to use. There was OBS from a Nike project, feathers from Victoria's Secret, a lacquer finish from Asprey, as well as push pins, rubber bands, felt, flowers, jelly beans—and even wood."

The front and center part of this open booth was devoted to showing examples of the design firm's process with images in light boxes of a Nike roll-out project and others. This was achieved via four images working in conjunction with Design Compendium's custom made design process books.

It took many hours to assemble the textured stripes for the background but they did allow visitors to the booth to "see and touch our creative solutions—making something extraordinary out of the ordinary."

DESIGN COMPENDIUM
design
production
installation
ZERO3

DESIGN COMPENDIUM
design
production
installation

OBJECTS OF ENVY

Architectural Digest Home Design Show,
    Pier 94, New York, NY
Design and Construction: *The Displayers,*
    New York, NY
Designer: *Stuart Anthony*
Photography: *Courtesy of The Displayers*

In a 10 ft. by 20 ft. space at the Architectural Digest Home Design show that took place at Pier 94 in New York, NY, The Displayers designed and built this simple but effective exhibit for Objects of Envy.

"The design goal was to create an environment that would attract attention from both directions on the main aisles surrounding the small booth space. The 'windowed wall' created white frames around the brightly-colored individual glass pieces—viewable from both sides of the booth." Since this was the client's first appearance at a trade show and the investment for creating a booth was a major factor, The Displayers incorporated standard materials into simple components that could easily and quickly be installed at the show site—or expanded for future and perhaps larger spaces. The freestanding pedestals and moveable table can also be repositioned or adapted to other configurations.

Confex Show, London, UK
Design and Fabrication: *Nomadic Display, London, UK*
Designer: *Gaven Parson*
Photography: *Apollo Photography, London, UK*

As a manufacturer of modular display units, Nomadic Display had to not only introduce itself and its three separate product lines but also make a lasting impression as a source for the attendees at the Confex show in London.

In a rather confined 335 sq. ft., Nomadic presented their Instand, Design Line and Platinum products/services along with printed graphics and lightweight fabric elements. The design called for a shiny white floor—raised up from the expo floor level—and a color palette of yellow, yellow-green and grass green on white. Four white columns supported the swirling patterned ring that

contained the central core of the exhibit stand. This crowning cornice was made of printed fabric stretched over an aluminum frame. Semi-round partitions, also white and brilliantly patterned in the chosen colors, carried the graphics and the copy that explained who Nomadic Design was and what they do.

A small information counter, up front, contained brochures and take-away literature and it was attached to one of the supporting columns. Plasma screens, on the main counter within the core, showed off some of Nomadic Display's work.

VK MOBILE

China High-Tech Fair 2005, Shenzhen, China
Design & Fabrication: *Shenzhen Pico*
       Exhibition Services Co. Ltd., Michael Yang
Photography: *Courtesy of Pico Shenzhen*

VK is a young but energetic South Korean company that wants to actively cultivate a larger share of the growing Chinese mobile phone market. For their appearance at the China High-Tech Fair in Shenzhen, China, VK asked the Pico Shenzhen Exhibition Company to design and fabricate "a magnificent and professional booth to promote the company image and arouse brand awareness" in the 400 sq. ft. allotted space.

The booth's design is centered on an arc shaped structure that has been combined with a "beeline" structure and together they "perfectly combine the company's image and product in one". To make the space seem larger and to add a "sense of clarity," the design team selected mostly translucent materials. The VK logo appears in the company's signature orange color against the sunny sky-blue of the ceiling and the contrast of the orange and blue "embodies wholeness and energy." Heroic scaled and framed graphics are accentuated by fluorescent light and they add dimension to the space while "drawing attention to product endorsements." The center of the space features a collection of towering pillars and the newest VK products that are displayed in glass cabinets.

The booth's design includes a closed storage area and an open demonstration/meeting zone that meets the functional requirements of VK.

MOSS, INC. ....

Globalshop 2004 & Exhibitors Show 2004,
        Las Vegas, NV
Design: *Kevin McPhee*
Technical Design: *Danny Bois of Moss, Inc.*
Fabrication: *Moss, Inc.*
Photography: *Moss/Dana Esposito of Access*
        TCA & Einzig Photography, Inc.

How does an exhibit designer/fabricator sell himself at a show where he is one amongst many others also showing themselves off at their very best? Moss, Inc. required "a structure that drew attention to their capabilities and areas of expertise." To accomplish this, using a design created by Kevin McPhee, they built a large spiraling wall and an elegant double funnel central structure—all curves and swirls.

The curving wall—like a nautilus shell—was fabricated of a translucent stretch fabric that "gave a hint of the framework beneath." The structure was fully revealed when the curtain was flipped away. The fabric was printed with a watery pattern that helped further the

sea-like imagery. Most surfaces of the booth were inkjet sublimation printed. The swirl continued into the 20 ft. by 20 ft. stand to become the service counter of the space. Rising up behind it were two elegant funnel shapes of the same fabric covered framework and these were "invisibly" supported from above. "The double funnel structure highlighted Moss' graphic mapping techniques by showing a continuous image around the funnel." The translucent funnel that surrounded the thinner cloud-like shape furthered the airiness created by the printed image and also affected a rather spa-like atmosphere: unusual on the hectic and frenetic trade show floor.

The checkerboard floor—in the two shades of cool blue that was used on the printed fabric—completed the design. Moss, Inc. won an outstanding achievement award in the Exhibit/Tradeshow booth category for this design from the Industrial Fabric Association International.

MOSS, INC.

Globalshop 2005, Las Vegas, NV
Design: *Mark Daniel of Slate*
Graphic Design: *Sean Semingen of Bamboo*
World Wide
Fabrication: *Moss, Inc.*
Photography: *Oscar Einzig, Einzig Photography.*

Fabric ribbon walls arched over the 20 ft. by 20 ft. space occupied by Moss, Inc. at Globalshop 2005 in Las Vegas. Fabricated by Moss, Inc., 2 in. square aluminum tubing was used for the framework that was covered with printed Spandex fabric and these panels also supported the booth's lighting system.

Standing as sentries to the white floored space were four curved display units –"demo curves"—with the colorful printing and integrated shelves that allowed Moss to demonstrate how stretch fabric structures can be used as a backdrop for product presentation. The printing on each unit was produced from another texture of Spandex fabric and all the printing made use of Moss' in-house, Ultra Print IDS printing technology. A curved Spandex-covered counter, accompanied by stools, filled the inner space and hanging lamps, supported by the arches, high-lighted the central area.

In this attractive design Moss was able to promote their capability with square and round tube framing, the curves that were possible and the firm's printing capabilities. This booth was recognized with the Award of Merit for Best Booth in the Visual Merchandising pavilion at Globalshop.

NEC

Equipotel, Sao Paulo, Brazil
Designer: *Jose Eduardo da Costa & Daniel Trotta*
Fabrication: *Eme Montagem, Sao Paulo, Brazil*
Photography: *Estilo Fotos*

NEC of Brazil is a producer of chemical products for cellulose and paper. For their appearance at the Equipotel Show in Sao Paulo, Brazil, they commissioned Jose Eduardo da Costa and Daniel Trotta to create their 550 sq. ft. stand. Though Equipotel is the biggest fair held in Brazil for Hotel & Restaurant Suppliers—the expo hall is not air conditioned. NEC chose to air-condition their space and thus an enclosed exhibit resulted.

The booth, constructed by Eme Montagem, projected the feeling of "movement." The lateral walls were

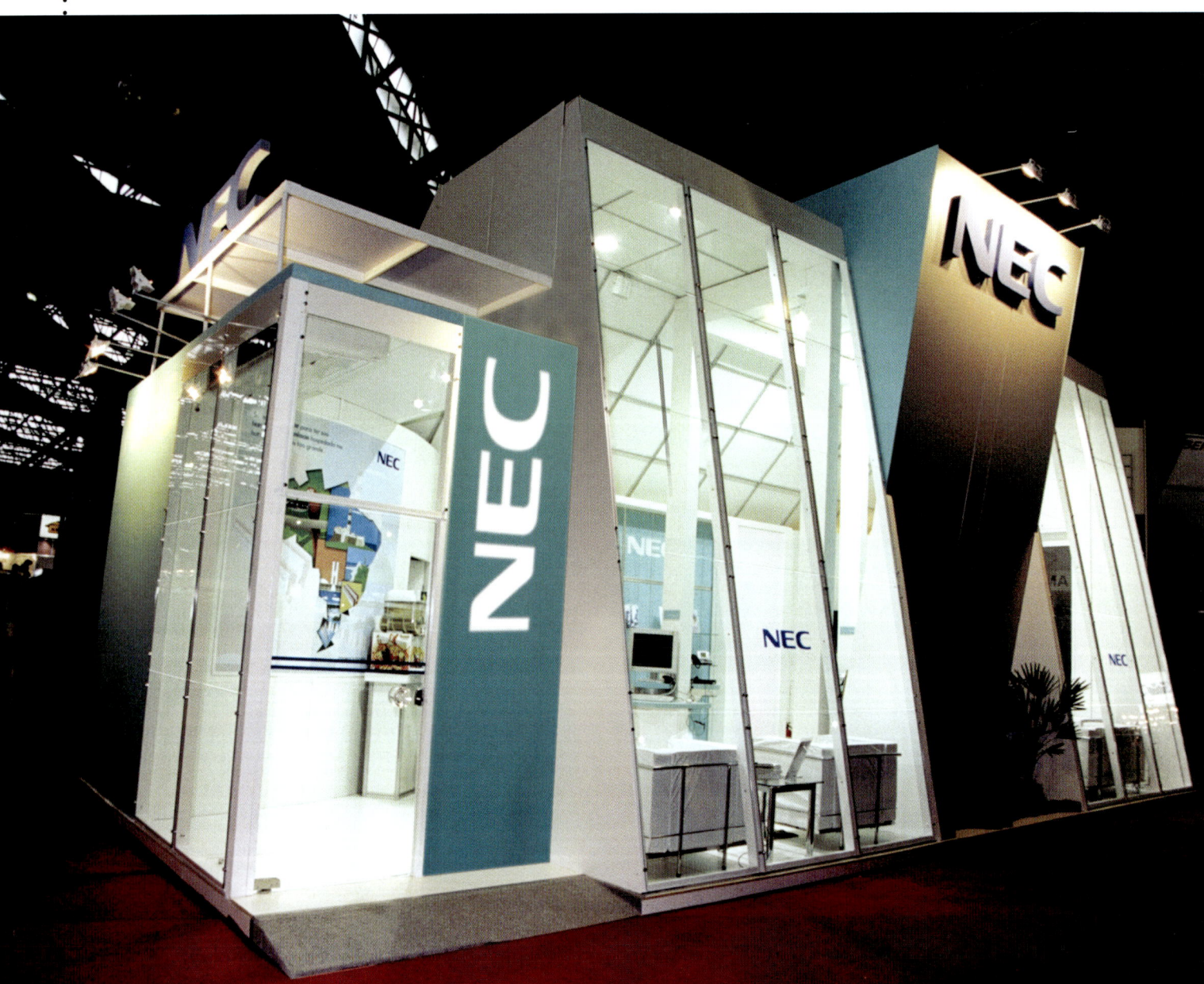

constructed of wood covered with a white vinyl material. The construction was interrupted by large areas of angled steel and glass panels. While the central solid area, covered in metallic silver and carrying the NEC logo on top, angled forward as it swept upwards, the glazed panels to either side sloped inwards as they ascended. Through the expanses of glass, attendees could see the activity and the presentation that was going on inside the enclosure. Throughout, NEC's signature colors of blue, white and silver appeared.

The interior of the stand was divided into three separate zones for conferencing and hospitality. Each area was furnished with comfortable chairs and a small bar counter. The NEC products were displayed in these "informal environments" where the clients were "hosted" by NEC's representatives.

CPFL ENERGIA

Expomanagement, Sao Paulo, Brazil
Designer: *Andre Roque Matheus & Daniel Trotta*
Fabrication: *Eme Montagem, Sao Paulo, Brazil*
Photography: *Estilo Fotos*

550 SQUARE FEET

For the Expomanagement trade show in Sao Paulo, Brazil, CPFL—an energy producing company—challenged Andre Roque Matheus and Daniel Trotta to create an exciting exhibit design for their 550 sq. ft. space. The big question was—"how much illumination is necessary to present 'energy'?" The main purpose for exhibiting was for CPFL to show how their "generation and distribution net combined with on-line technology makes getting information about energy distribution quick and easy."

The design, executed by Eme Montagem, consisted of three walls and a spacious opening off the aisle. The white wood floor and the walls covered in white vinyl fabric created the desired "clean" look. The aluminum-framed Spandex panels added a "sense of freedom and movement" and also complemented the swath of blue vinyl that carried the company's name and logo over the entry. Adding interest, up front, was the blue light emanating from beneath the blue acrylic panels set into the floor.

In addition to the blue framed panels on the walls that provided the information about energy distribution, the designers also included two small, interactive work stations and a small conferencing area. According to the design/construction team, "Thus, visitors could get straight information from the three informative boards installed in the stand which is brightly illuminated and creates a clear, transparent environment."

PIRELLI

570 SQUARE FEET

Auto Salon 2005, Makuhari Exhibit Hall, Japan
Designer: *Takehiko Uemura*
Design & Fabrication: *Pico International
    Ltd., Japan*
Photography: *Courtesy of Pico Japan*

Pico Japan executed Takehiko Uemura's vision for Pirelli's 570 sq. ft. space at the Auto Salon 2005 that took place in the Makuhari Exhibit Hall. The concept was simple: Pirelli is all about tires and tires are round—rubber donuts—so let's pile up the tires/donuts for an effect.

The entire display consists of a series of these stacks of abstract tires made of wood and covered with carpeting material. They are set off-kilter for effect—and a purpose. The purpose was so that the lighting set on the

undersurfaces of some of the "tires" would reflect down and create interesting glows or haloes. The backlit Pirelli logo appeared on some of the pileups and each pile was of a different height. One of the piles with the Pirelli logo on top swept out to become the information counter at one corner of the stand.

The actual tires were presented vertically—like they would be used—rather than horizontally. Thus, they contrasted with the exhibit "tires." Brightly-illuminated by a ring of lamps set into a suspended Pirelli-branded ring, the tire treads could be truly appreciated.

The play of soft rounded shapes, the subtle color variations and the highlights and shadows created by the lighting plan made this a memorable booth.

E-MOBILE

Wireless Show 2005, Tokyo, Japan
Design & Fabrication: *Pico International Ltd., Japan*
Designers: *Takahiro Suzuki & Kensuke Tsutsui*
Project Executive: *Hiroshi Arashima*
Photography: *Yutaka Okada*

570 SQUARE FEET

E-mobile made a striking appearance at the Wireless Show 2005 in Tokyo, Japan in a 570 sq. ft. space. The booth was designed and fabricated by Pico Japan. E-mobile's red, white and blue logo set the palette for the design that was only partially contained by a single wall.

A central element rose up to 16 ft. and the white illuminated superstructure carried the giant "e" and "m" letters in red and blue. A red panel construction served as the focal element behind a platform where presentations/demonstrations were performed. "Leaning" fixtures were provided for the attendees here. The red enclosure also served as a storage space for materials and such.

The opposite side of the central construction consisted of a raised red counter upon which e-mobile products were shown—and were available for testing. Raised up from the counter were several flat screen monitors upon which company messages were relayed and attendees could also "see" the demonstrations on these screens.

The single blue wall that ran along one side of the space supported the explanatory charts and pictographs that explained and extolled the e-mobile products. A projecting cornice, also blue, carried the spotlights that illuminated the information panels. The logo-red floor pulled the space together as an entity on the exhibition hall floor.

DEKLA

Interior Design Show 2005, Toronto, ON
Design: *ll BY lV Design, Toronto, ON*
Photography: *David Whittaker*

Dekla brought together Scavolini Kitchens and Agape Bathrooms in their 600 sq. ft. space at the Interior Design Show in Toronto. To introduce these new lines by the celebrated Italian design firms, Dekla called upon ll BY lV Design of Toronto to create a simple setting that would help to advance the new products being presented.

The task, according to Dan Menchion of ll BY lV was "to create a display that allows the absolutely gorgeous products to speak for themselves." To do this, the designers built a semi-surround with a wide cuffed overhead fascia suspended from above, Standing out from what looked like rippling water was the Scavolini logo on one side of the hanging roof and the Agape name on the other. The inside of this cuff was white and splattered with Italian words in red that described the new products displayed below. They added to the flavor of the imported products while adding a colorful accent to the monochromatic merchandise below. The exhibit space was comprised basically of two walls: one with a

red tile exterior facing the back aisle and another in the center of the stand that served as a separation between the "kitchen" and the "bathroom" while also supporting the products for both "rooms." These mosaic tiled walls shimmered under the lights from above.

The dramatic "kitchen" furnished with Scavolini's Crystal design filled one area while on the other side of the

central wall was the black and white Agape bathroom fixtures including the Spoon tub which was set in the center of the "bathroom."

The booth was located just inside the front doors of the show and the impact of the red and blue overhead façade served to further dramatize the black and white product presentation that could be viewed from three sides.

WINNTECH ....

600 SQUARE FEET

Globalshop 2004, Las Vegas, NV
Design & Fabrication: *Winntech, Kansas City, MO*
Creative Director: *Brian Harvey*
Art Director: *Stephanie Malcy*
Design Team: *Adam Herbig/Matt Johnson/*
  Jeremy Meyer
Photography: *Alistair Tutton, Photography*

It was a matter of money—and also doing something so different—so unique—so "way out" that it would be very "way in" and the talk of Globalshop 2004 in Las Vegas. Winntech was there to once again introduce themselves as designers/fabricators of interactive fixtures, store interiors and retail merchandising specialists. They settled on oranges—thousands of them!

A truss was suspended over the 20 ft. by 30 ft. space. Suspended from this ring were over a thousand

orange-y oranges. "There was a method to this madness as we added brand imagery in the floor covering—a giant white 20 ft. diameter carpet, and it was used as a large format floor graphic upon which we listed our core services and their applications." And—orange is the new "hot," "in" color!

Brand iconography was built into the meeting area fixtures which were located at the four corners of the booth. Here custom orange-colored seats and tables were provided. Using large, backlit projections, dynamic signage presentations were thrown onto the truss system overhead. The sale representatives were dressed in white coveralls, branded in orange, and accented with orange athletic shoes.

After the show was pulled and the oranges—figuratively—squeezed, Winntech used the "agent orange" theme as a followup for marketing campaigns. "It formed a definitive brand statement that our clients were able to associate with our name."

LAMIN-ART

**Woodworking & Furnishing Suppliers
(AWFS) 2005, Las Vegas, NV**
Design: *Paul Fujihara, Outhouse Design*
Fabrication: *GES Exposition Services:
Matt Heinze and staff*
Tension Fabric Structure: *Transformit,
New York, NY*
Photography: *Gary Michael*

The sweeping arc of fabric pulled over an aluminum frame is "swiss-cheesed" with opening holes that gave attendees a look into the 600 sq. ft. space occupied by Lamin-Art. Lamin-Art is a U.S. based supplier of premium high pressure laminates and with this exhibit, designed by Paul Fugihara of Outhouse Design and

executed by GES Exposition Services, they sought to "redefine the conventional view of laminate as a flat surfacing material." Here the laminates are presented on curved surfaces! "To reinforce the curved surface theme, sweeping white curvilinear tension fabric walls (by Transformit) defined the product display areas." Within the 20 ft. by 30 ft. space, 6 in. and 10 in. diameter tubes were wrapped with some of Lamin-Art's newest materials.

These product displays showed the users of laminates that it was possible to achieve this degree of curvature. "Post-forming grade laminate is a 'special order' item so a longer lead time is required. By using a vertical grade in this application, Lamin-Art showed their customers the versatility of their product." To achieve this effect, .028 in.

vertical-grade laminates were cold bent around plywood tubes. Three different finishes of Lamin-Art were used at the workstations in the booth.

This exhibit stand received an honorable mention "Showstopper Award" at the AWFS fair.

NOKIA EXPERIENCE CENTER

600 SQUARE FEET

Traveling Exhibit
Design: *Fitch:RPA, Powell, OH*
Creative Director: *Lynn Rosenbaum*
Strategist: *Lisa Cook*
Director of Implementation For NOKIA:
    Randy Miller
Media Relations Manager: *Winston Wright*
Sr. Marketing Manager: *Winston Wright*
Fabrication: *Exhibitgroup/Giltspur, TX*
Photography: *Brandon King, Fitch:RPA*

Twenty five Nokia Experience Centers, designed by Fitch:RPA of Powell, OH and fabricated by Exhibit-group/Giltspur of Texas, have been rolled out in malls across the U.S. Mobile communication devices are currently being sold solely through service providers and on those service providers own terms. "There is much more to our brand and our company than service providers—with their limited resources—have been able to convey." The Experience Center will augment their vending capabilities," said Winston Wright, Sr. retail planning & merchandising director for Nokia.

In developing the Experience Center, Fitch:RPA harnessed the lifestyle driven brand that Nokia has built. Nothing is sold in the Center, rather it helps consumers to "make a tangible and visceral connection with Nokia's products and brands." The 20 ft. by 30 ft. unit that evolved is a freestanding, glass walled structure complete with its own raised floor, ceiling and contained lighting. While inside this exhibit, the visitor is "ensconced in Nokia's world—surrounded by lights, sounds, displays and imagery of Nokia." These centers are located within malls and they feed off the energy generated by the locations. The transparent walls, perforated ceilings and ramps "allow the flow of the mall's ambient sounds and sights" while the ramp "creates a sense of one leaving one world and entering another."

Warm, cool colors and tones are used and the ambience combines high technology and contemporary design with classical elements and wood. The sharp, modern angular design "effectively complements the highly-stylized and technologically-advanced mobile communication products" featured within. Each product is individually highlighted and displayed: each phone lit from the ceiling. An internally illuminated acrylic button holds the phone and creates its own sense of energy. The button rotates 360 degrees, is freestanding and simple—and allows visitors to see the phone from all angles. Curved tables in the middle of the space allow people to congregate and spend more time in the Center. The open wall spaces and the centralized displays allow visitors to freely walk around each phone fixture. The phone displays are live and thus interactive. Internet access is also provided so that visitors may search the Nokia website for local service providers that carry the desired phones.

ALU

Globalshop 2005, Las Vegas, NV
Design: *Jay Haws, ALU and Bloom Interior*
       Architecture, Callison Architecture and
       Pavlik Design Team
Fabrication: *ALU, New York, NY*
Photography: *Courtesy of ALU*

ALU, a designer/manufacturer of modular merchandising systems, exhibit construction systems and store fixtures, took a unique approach to showing off the versatility of their systems at Globalshop in Las Vegas. In addition to the firm's own in-house design team, they called upon three architectural design firms to "add their interpretive values to the presentation of the ALU product." These firms were "challenged to interpret ALU systems in innovative ways, with the general direction of ALU's catalogue theme—'Nothing is what it seems.'"

Each design firm had a separate space within the booth to express themselves.

Bloom Interior Architecture came up with a wrapped, angulated concept that emphasized the flexibility of the Box, Wall and Reed wall mount systems. "We treated ALU as a skeletal system which provides structure for what lives beneath the surface The fabric treatment is representative of skin, which protects the system, transforming sharp lines into soft silhouettes." The designers used the graphic pattern "Synaptic Bliss" designed by Aziz + Cusher of New York, NY as the cellular layer beneath the skin. "The presence of light represents life."

The designers at Callison Architecture of Seattle featured a hanging platform, provided by Urban Hardwoods, in their allotted space. It served as a complement to the simple, light components of the Acrobat system. "The system made us supremely aware of gravity and the inherent potential energy stored within. Our design explores this gravitational relationship by challenging our sense of weight and weightlessnes."

The Box system was used by Pavlik Design Team of Ft. Lauderdale to create an architectural retail environment that "emphasized light, space and singular product presentation that can be utilized for either a self-service environment, bold graphical presentation or full retail application."

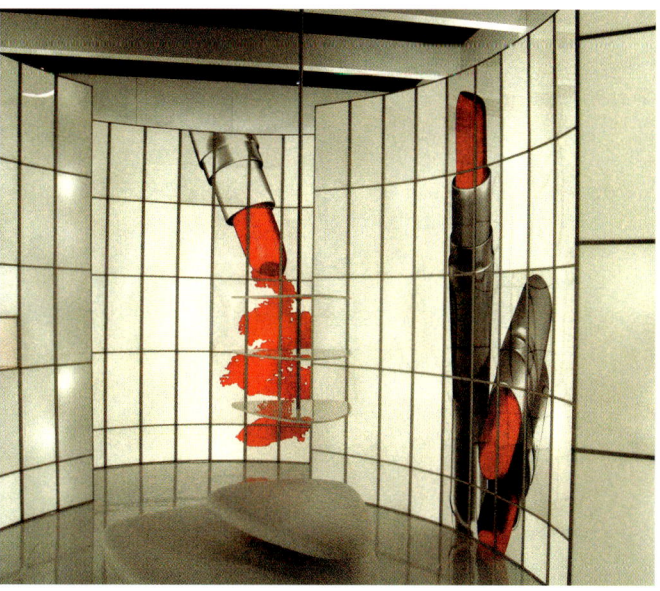

REYNOLDS COMPOSITES

800 SQUARE FEET

InterBike Show, Las Vegas, NV
Design: *Mauk Design, Mitchell Mauk*
Fabrication: *Reynolds Composites, Ferrari Color*
Photography: *Courtesy of Mauk Design*

Since the InterBike Show in Las Vegas is the major show for the U.S. Bicycle industry and since Reynolds Composites manufactures carbon fiber wheels, tubing and components for bicycles, it was only natural that Reynolds would want to make a big impression in their 800 sq. ft. stand at the show.

Mitchell Mauk of Mauk Design created this display. "The design distilled the Reynolds image into a space as simple as we could make it. There was nothing in the exhibit space except product and brand. The back wall showed a bicycle rider not on a bike but on an array of Reynolds' components—'flying in formation.' This was key to drawing the distinction between a component manufacturer and a bike manufacturer."

The only products displayed were wheel-sets: carbon fiber on the yellow stand and aluminum wheels on the red stand. All the wheels were rotating—in motion—and inside the displays were the motors that moved the wheels at various speeds. Visitors were able to pick up and examine these rotating wheels. "The result was a display that spoke to the soul of a bicyclist as well as bringing a certain amount of poetic motion to a macho product."

The exhibit drew a high-tech frame around the products by using clean, whiter space, product movement, good lighting and color. The designers used vinyl inkjet output stretched over a recycled carbon fiber frame that was constructed from rejected Reynolds sailboard masts. The flooring was snap-together antifatigue matting. The wheel displays were fabricated out of sheet aluminum. "The exhibit was visible as a clean, glowing beacon surrounded by the clutter of competition stands."

SYNGENTA

860 SQUARE FEET

Expoprag, Sao Paulo, Brazil
Design: *Fabio Schiavon*
Fabrication: *Eme Mointagem, Sao Paulo*
Photography: *Polly Studios*

"How can we have our client interacting with a product for urban plague control?" That may seem like a weird question to ask but since Fabio Schiavon and Eme Montagem were challenged by Syngenta to create a booth for this producer of pesticides at Expoprag in Sao Paulo, it was completely relevant. The "answer" or "solution" was to create an interactive game in the 860 sq. ft. space.

Visitors were handed "joy sticks" as they entered and with these they were supposed to "kill the plague pests." To enhance the game-like ambiance, the floor was made up of a series of alternating blue carpet and white rubber tile rings. "To create an environment of curiosity and pleasure," the designers emphasized a color palette of blue, yellow and purple. A sweeping awning of yellow and white striped canvas flowed back from the stand's entry to the rear wall of the space. There was a large cutout in the center of this "roof" that was filled with a metal grid that supported backlit graphic panels. Since this booth was located on the lower of the two levels of the exhibition hall, visitors on the upper level could get glimpses of the "fun and games" going on in the Syngenta stand through that cutout in the ceiling.

Plasma screens were embedded in the side walls for educational and entertainment value while futuristic tables and demo stands—in yellow and white and accented in blue—were set out on the "bull's-eye" patterned floor. Here visitors could interact with the Syngenta products and the company's representatives.

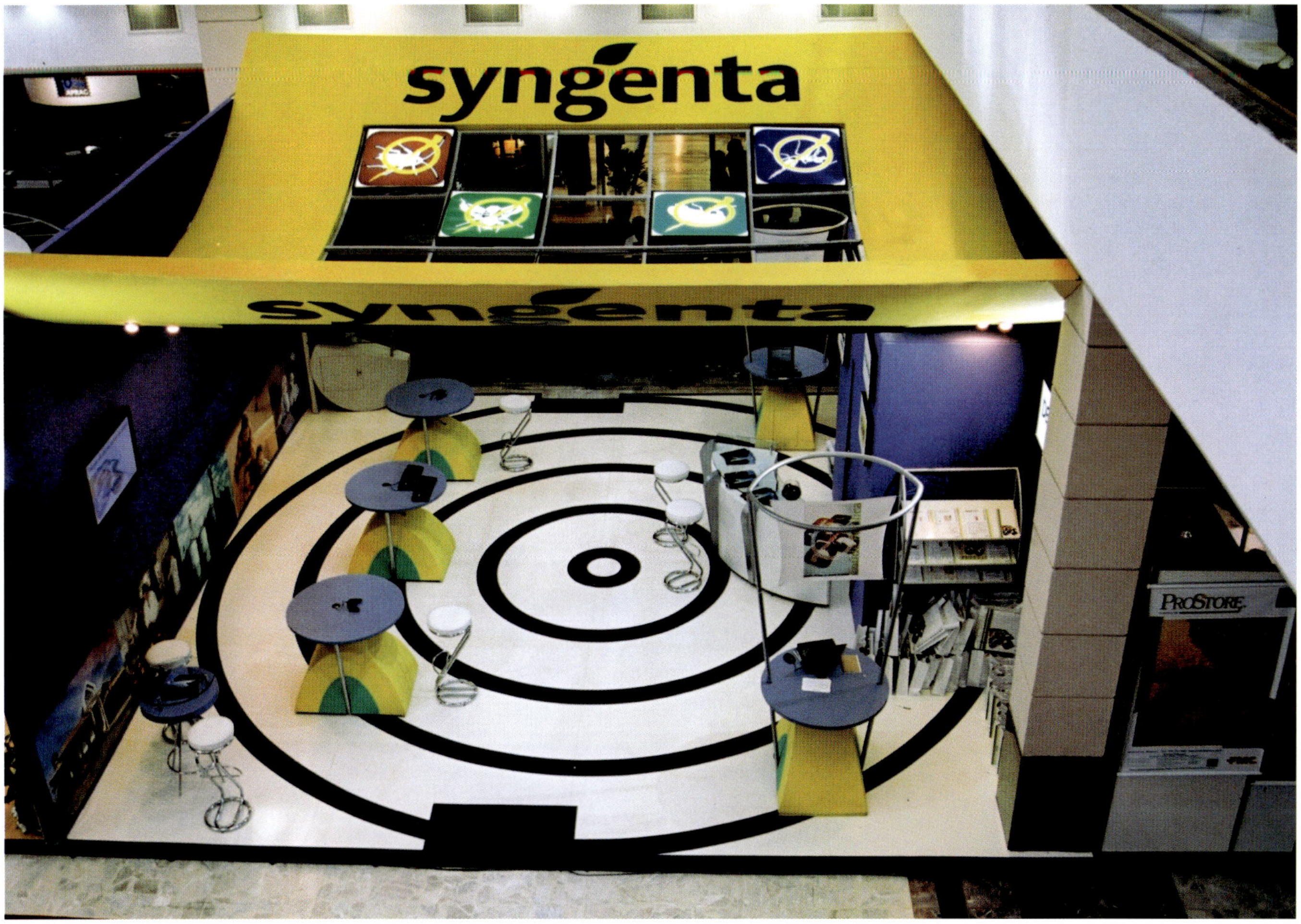

PLANTRONICS

CES: Consumer Electronics Show 2004,
Las Vegas, NV
Design: *Czarnowski Ltd.*
Fabrication: *Czarnowski & Transformit*
Photography: *Line 8 Photography*

900 SQUARE FEET

To let the attendees know that Plantronics is the world's leading designer/manufacturer/distributors of light-weight communication headset products, the company commissioned Czarnowski to create an eye-filling 900 sq. ft. exhibit for the company's appearance at the CES Show in Las Vegas. According to the designers, this design was a radical change from Plantronics' previous trade show stands. "This design successfully employed vivid color, vibrant lifestyle graphics and dramatic light-

ing to make Plantronics' industry leadership obvious and unquestionable."

The designers used stretched fabric structures from Transformit's "Fascinating Rhythms" collection of catalogue solutions and had them customized with dye sublimated stretch fabric skins. These internally-illuminated towers with lifestyle graphics and the Plantronics' logo anchored the light-looking green Lucite demo tables set out on the patterned floor. The various headsets were presented on these outposts along with the explanatory copy. The changing light color effects—on the floor and on the units as well as the sweeping rear wall—"kept the environment active and interesting."

CALZADO CHRISTIAN GALLERY

Sapica 2005, Leon, Mexico
Design: *Arrca Exposiciones, Leon*
Creative Director: *Pablo Arreola Calleros Tsutsui*
Photography: *Ana Paula Arreola Calleros*

Shoes are BIG business in Mexico as exemplified by the Sapica Expo, a major trade show that takes place in Leon, Mexico. Leon is the capital of Mexico's giant shoe industry with many manufacturers and distributors based there. Calzado Christian Gallery was one of the numerous manufacturer/distributors with a stand at the show and their aim was to have their 950 sq. ft. stand not only attractive—but attracting.

The façade of the stand rose up two stories high and the sharply-angled panels that jutted forward from the aisle line added to the sense of movement and verticality of the design. The balance of the stand's facade consisted of a semitransparent fabric skin stretched over a metal grid framework. Openings to either side of the sharp angular up-front projection led into the open space. Visitors passed under the overhanging mezzanine and the stairs that connected the V.I.P. conference/showroom above. This, too, was a grid framework covered with translucent panels; the framing served as the fixture displays for the shoes shown there.

The expo level space was furnished with glass topped tables and white chairs and the perimeter walls were lined with angled shelf units upon which the new men's shoes were displayed against white translucent panels. The showcase fixtures were separated by the signature red colored fins and the fixtures were interspersed with 4 ft. by 8 ft. backlit transparencies of male-oriented lifestyle images. Punctuating the space were several two story high logo graphic panels with brand images and the company's name.

NOKIA (THAILAND) LTD.

1,050 SQUARE FEET

Commart & Commtech Show 2004
     Queen Sirikit National Convention
     Center, Bangkok, Thailand
Design & Fabrication: *Pico (Thailand) Public Co, Ltd.*
Project Director: *Vivat Rongkavong*
Project Manager: *Akkapol Panyadilok*
Project Executive: *Jaruwan Koedamrong*
Construction & Graphic Designer: *Janat*
     Thiengsurin
Photography: *Courtesy of Pico Thailand*

The two-level high exhibit designed and constructed by Pico Thailand for Nokia Thailand made a standout appearance at the Commart & Commtech Show in the Queen Sirikit National Convention Center in Bangkok. The 1,050 sq.ft. space was accentuated by its striking black lacquered construction.

Four 20 ft. high black laminate panels rose up from the gaily striped floor and they carried the Nokia message: "Business," "Music & Lifestyle" and "Imagine." The fourth panel served to highlight the Nokia logo and proclaim the theme of the exhibit: Life, Work and Play. Units up front—off the aisle—carried brochures and samples of the many Nokia products that attendees were invited to interact with. During the show hours—at specified times—live models wearing the appropriate lifestyle outfits were visible on the raised platform behind the four black panels. They were shown using the assorted Nokia products and further emphasized the exhibit's theme. At other times, this raised second level of the booth was used for conferencing and hospitality.

To offset the black finish of the pylons and the perimeter walls, the floors were highlighted with colored ribbons of blue, green, yellow and orange inlay vinyl. These same bright colors dominated the graphics used throughout. LED lighting was combined with expanses of backlit translucent panels on some of the interior walls of the ground level of the booth. Lined up in front of one of these walls were rows of bottles filled with colored liquid that once again restated the major ascent colors of the exhibit.

DHL

InterModal, Sao Paulo, Brazil
Design: *Elcio Pires*
Fabrication: *Eme Montagem, Sao Paulo*
Photography: *Zilene Rolin*

1,200 SQUARE FEET

Over 350 exhibitors filled the Center of Immigrant Exhibition Hall in Sao Paulo for the annual InterModal South America Expo. The exhibit covered 22,000 sq. meters of space with exhibits for companies involved in marine, road, rail and air transportation as well as the manufacturers that service this industry. Danzas and DHL joined up for this event and part of the challenge for Elcio Pires and Eme Montagem was to emphasize the new logo of this joint effort. Also, the two-level exhibit, in a 1,200 sq. ft. space, had to show off the three services provided by the company: DHL Express, DHL Solutions and DHL Air & Ocean. The lower, or floor level, was devoted to introducing the company's services while the upper level was reserved for conferencing with potential clients.

Yellow was added to the already recognizable red signature of DHL. The striking new color was added behind the red letters of the logo and the yellow was also used as an accent on the walls and on the floating elements of the design. White was used extensively to open up the space and to highlight the red and yellow colors. Mahogany wood was added to the palette and appeared as an accent throughout and on the stairs that led to the upper level. The wood was added "to create a most harmonious atmosphere."

The ground level was furnished with informal white bistro tables and chairs to accommodate visitors who could visit the educational exhibits arranged on the floating panels located in the area under the mezzanine. The upper level was divided into three "rooms" and the separating semitransparent panels offered privacy without "the feeling of weight or enclosure." Each room served an other of the three services provided by the joining of Danzas and DHL.

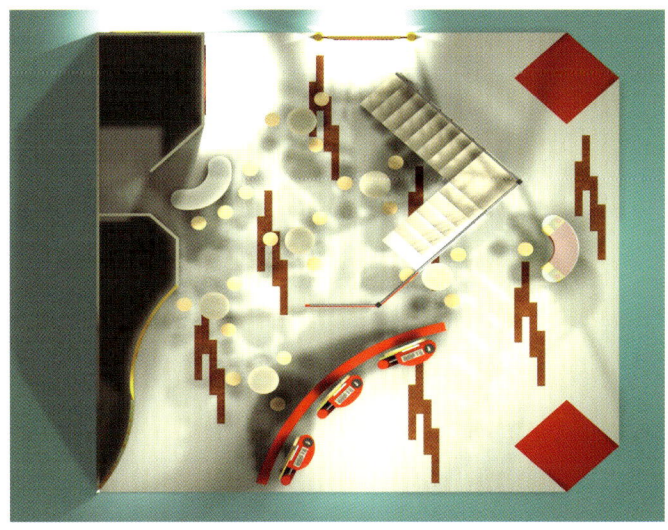

LEVI'S CLOTHESLINE

1,200 SQUARE FEET

Clothes Show, London, 2004
Design: *Checkland Kindleyside, London, UK*
Account Executive: *Henry Barnes*
Principal Designer: *Joe Evans*
Design Team: *Carl Murch & Clare Orrell*
Project Managers: *Hana Carter & Richard Dunkin*
Photography: *Adrian Wilson*

The UK had yet to see "the feminine side" of what is traditionally viewed as a masculine brand, so when Levi's launched its "For Girls" line at the Clothes Show in London, they called upon the retail design firm they have worked with for many years.

Checkland Kindleyside, of London, had just completed a prototype store design for Levi's first Girl's store, in Paris, and the designers took their design cues from that design for this 1,200 sq, ft., space.

Showcasing an offer catering exclusively to the young, style-conscious and "sassy" female market, the design concept was entirely curvaceous and hand-crafted with hand-stenciled graphics. The designers created "an architecturally impressive exhibition space which is interactive from both the outside and in. On approach, it is akin to walking into a forest. You get glimpses through its perimeter as you queue to enter the space." The entire space was constructed of over nine ft. tall, spray stenciled cardboard cylinders "which allowed a vcurvaceous flowing and unique shape." They were "custom designed for the exhibition space and, wrapping around the architectural elements, allowed interesting elements to be added." 300 mm cardboard tubes were cut down to be used as seats while 1,200 mm tubes served as dressing rooms in the stand.

LEVI'S CLOTHESLINE

The stand was into product concepts including Lady Levi's, 501 Jeans and Levi's Red Tab Jeans. There was also a Clothes show exclusive discount section for the Show customers. Each concept area was treated with a unique signature of sprayed symbols. Products were presented on simple, two-level red hang rods and they were highlighted by a featured hanging garment above, and the brand identification. The hang rods were supported by red merchandise towers in which the jeans were folded. This merchandising technique was originally produced for the Girl's shop in Paris and has been adapted to other areas in retail stores where the Girl's jeans are now offered.

In addition to the exhibit, Checkland Kindleysides prepared the entire promotional campaign that included press invitations, press packs, take-away stickers and T-shirts encased within cardboard tubes.

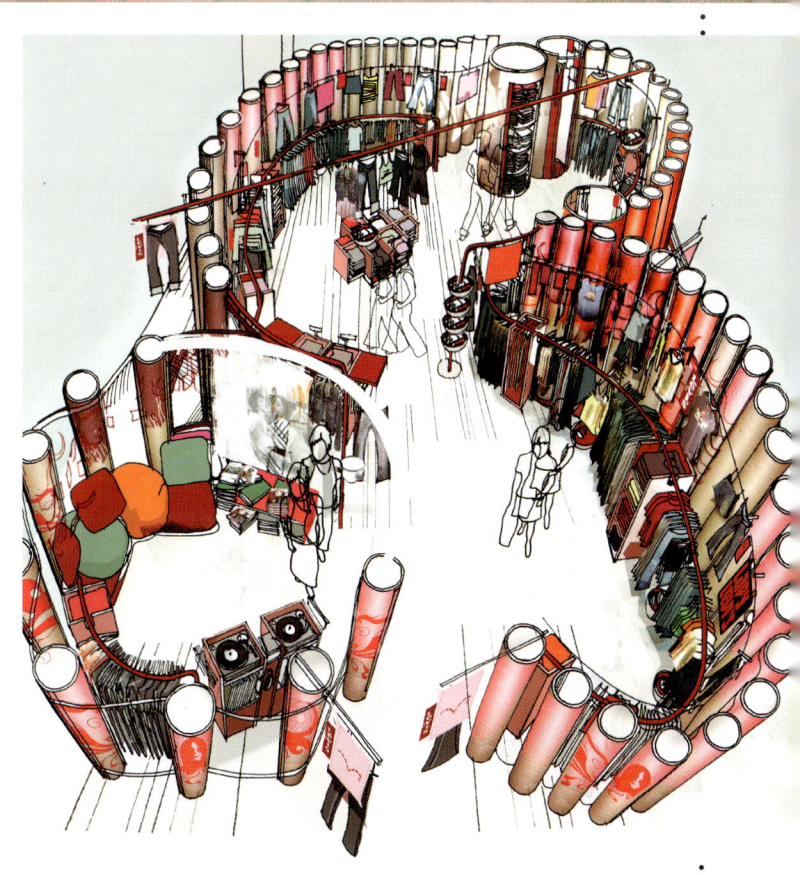

HENNIEZ

Gastronomia 2004, Lausanne, Switzerland
Design & Fabrication: *Syma Systems*
Photography: *Courtesy of Syma Systems*

To celebrate its forthcoming 100th jubilee, Henniez, the well known and bestselling mineral water producer in Switzerland, commissioned Syma Systems to create its booth in the 1,200 sq. ft. space at Gastronomia 2004 in Lausanne, Switzerland

Syma not only designs exhibits but it also produces many exhibit construction modular systems and for this design they used a Syma two-story basic structure along with the Syma Molto 150 system. A light-filled ceiling of fabric stretched over the Syma modular system was partially supported by the 20 ft. tall graphic panels that were also printed on fabric and stretched over the

structural framework. These illuminated panel/walls semi enclosed the stand and there were wide openings on all sides that allowed visitors to freely enter and move about. The major interior elements were the bar and the bar stools and they were surrounded by lightweight aluminum tables and chairs. The purpose of the exhibit was to have guests come in and sample the Henniez products which included other drinks and fruit juices.

The pale aqua/turquoise and cool blue corporate Henniez colors along with white—provided the appropriate background for the "Natural Sparkle" campaign and the products being featured. Among the highlighted items were the 50 cc bottle for a single serving and the 75 cc bottle which would be ideal for two to share. These were on view with other new products in glass topped museum cases that were lined up in the center of the wood floored space and viewable from the bar and the table seating. More museum cases flanked the two, two story high graphic panels.

1,270 SQUARE FEET

Bread & Butter Berlin 2005, Berlin, Germany
Design: *Checkland Kindleysides*
Photography: *Courtesy of Checkland Kindleysides*

Bread & Butter Berlin is a trade show of "contemporary fashion attire of the highest order: premium denims, designer and high-end fashion plus exclusive women's wear and menswear labels." For their appearance at this show, Levi's had a dual booth display designed for them by Checkland Kindleysides. In one area they focused on showing Levi's Red and Levi's Vintage clothing—the premium lines. In the second space at the show—the Spirit Room—a lounge was created where guests could relax, socialize and view key pieces of other Levi's collections and also preview the latest TV campaigns.

"Taking tailoring as a thread, we used photography from Levi's archives of pattern cutting, manufacturing and production as inspiration for the exhibition." Garment patterns were digitally printed onto oiled oak panels and

these serve as the backgrounds for key garments. Adjacent oversized, high gloss colored photographs leaned against the interior perimeter walls. Based on an actual cutting room table, a high level horizontal surface sliced through this space. Models walked on this runway or catwalk and they could be seen from many areas in the exhibition hall. This high counter also served as a lay-down surface for garment display.

The Spirit Room was highlighted by a red neon light and was physically removed from the previously described space. "Using materials and a color palette echoing elements in that stand, we designed a space instilled with the 'spirit' of Levi's." Angled planes of black with bold "built for pioneers" statements contrasted with the white seating and the social area. Oiled oak panels were decorated with white, hand-stenciled graphics that were created from imagery used at the exhibition stand. Black and white photography "created nuances and a change in atmosphere between the two spaces."

Bread & Butter, Eurovision 2006,
Barcelona, Spain
Design: *Checkland Kindleysides, London, UK*
Photography: *Courtesy of Checkland Kindleysides*

"Levi's are the pioneers; the original, authentic denim manufacturers for over 150 years. Our concept plays to the cachet of the brand and gives the product an iconic, almost spiritual status." Thus spoke the creative design team at London-based Checkland Kindleysides as they prepared the trade show exhibit for Levi's Bread & Butter stand at Eurovision 2006 in Barcelona, Spain.

The concept called for a plain, simple oak corral and the perimeter displayed many of Levi's "firsts" in accomplishments and denim. Breaks in the wood outer wall were filled with smoked glass and featured Levi's Two-Horse badge—"creating intrigue and allowing a glimpse into the exhibition inside." The inner space projected an "authentic, raw statement" and encouraged a seamless flow through the space. Photographic interpretations of the famous Two-Horse badge appeared about 7 ft. off the floor and were visible across the exhibition hall. Graphic images were used to provide visual references to the Levi's "firsts."

"Wooden blocks emulated Japanese prayer blocks; when hung with red string and printed with visuals and messages, they acted as navigational aids—highlighting the different Levi's sub-brands." In keeping with that, the designers developed a range of "shrines." One side acted as a method of visual merchandising to display the product and/or graphic while the other side was used to hang product. Live models sat on or inside, these "shrines"—"statue-like in appearance." Light boxes, set inside the perimeter wall created an altar-style setting while a large plasma screen played a Levi's black and white interleaved film "to entertain and add atmosphere."

"The interior was calm—a place for reflection. Smoked glass screens divided the space into dedicated areas to showcase Levi's products. Low seating with leather pillows, cork stools and tables provided a space to welcome guests. Relaxed and informal, the lounge emulated the look and feel of a gallery. A long oak bar served food and drink." A specially designed V.I.P. area with a Levi's signature red carpet, provided a luxurious retreat from the crowds at the show.

LINTEC ADVANCED TECHNOLOGY

SemiCon Taiwan, Taipei, Taiwan
Design: *Kingsmen, Taiwan*
Photography: *Courtesy of Kingsmen*

Having worked with Lintec Advanced Technology on previous exhibits, Kingsmen Taiwan's design team knew the client's objective and thus were able to design this 1,330 sq. ft. stand for the SemiCon show held in Taipei, Taiwan. The "creative yet functional" design replaced the actual machines that were previously used, with an open and spacious feeling that featured slim plasma screens and monitors, and glass paneled floors which displayed products and machine flow charts.

Suspended over the skeletal framework of the stand is a giant wood grid. The booth itself is a column and lintel construction with more overhead cross beams than vertical uprights. Between the uprights are self-supporting billboards with messages and monitors that tell the Lintec story. The blue, illuminated floor panels in the center suggest a pool and the pool is flanked with verdant foliage along the two long sides. Seating is provided on an "island" in the middle of the space.

The rear part of the stand is semi-enclosed with a two story high structure and the mezzanine level is used for hospitality and conferencing. It overlooks the "out of doors pool area." Messages and visuals were provided on both the inside of the skeletal construction as well as the traffic-facing exterior surfaces. The walls of the rear unit also carried messages and samples encased in oval shaped, illuminated shadow boxes. All in all—"a spacious and engaging environment."

CONTINUUM

ICSC, International Council of Shopping
      Centers, Las Vegas, NV
Design: *Lorenc + Yoo, Roswell, GA*
Collaborator: *Beth Cochran, Journey
      Communication, Wayne, PA*
Fabrication: *Feorge Freudiger, Geograph Ind., Inc*
Photography: *Rion Rizzo, Creative
      Sources Photography*

1,500 SQUARE FEET

Continuum is a division of Pioneer Companies and it is a full service national retail and office development firm. Continuum's mission is to create "livable people places" and to renovate outmoded malls into "open air Main Streets." To affect this concept for Continuum's booth at the ICSC Show in Las Vegas, the design team at Lorenc + Yoo of Roswell, GA created the illustrated exhibit design.

The 1,500 sq. ft. space has been divided into one major and two smaller conference rooms and the balance of the space was reserved for "the plaza," a poster gallery of projects and a casual dining area. The space, as a whole, has a "human touch" that has been enhanced by color and the aroma of fresh cut flowers. Through the use of a series of muted colors anchored with a color softened but masculine I-beam as a major design detail, "the space presented itself as an 'urban' gathering place." Two light posts with identifying banners appear at the entrances into the space.

The main conference rotunda space was the focal point of the exhibit design. The interior was dominated by a ceiling cone with a vertical light source and up-lighting sconces on each column. "The bouncing lighting allowed the entire space to glow." Since the glass partitions around this room were frosted to eye level and then clear above, the "roof seemed to float above the columns." There were pegs for presentation boards on the perimeter wall and the showing of multimedia presentations was facilitated by the cabinet in the center of the space.

65

WINNTECH

1,500 SQUARE FEET

GlobalShop 2005, Las Vegas, NV
Design & Fabrication: *Winntech, Kansas City, MO*
Creative Director: *Brian Harvey*
Design Team: *Matt Johnson & Jeremy Meyers*
Photography: *Alistyair Tutton Photography*

To follow up on their "oranges" bonanza at GlobalShop 2004, Winntech was pressured to come up with something new and different—but still capitalized—or "squeezed more juice" out of last year's orange cascade. "We knew that we wanted to accomplish some color association but also have a different feel to the presentation."

In the 1,500 sq. ft. space Winntech used a simple, extruded Lucite shape to create an enclosed lounge environment that provided a series of alternative presentation stations. The booth was really two skeletal cubes connected by an entry space and it had an almost toylike appearance. Visitors ascended a white ramp to enter into the space between the two cubes that made up the total exhibit. Suspended over the space –in the signature Winntech color—was the company's graphic/logo.

The frosted frames that were used were bound into self-standing units by the orange pipes that were threaded horizontally through the frames at their tops and bottoms.

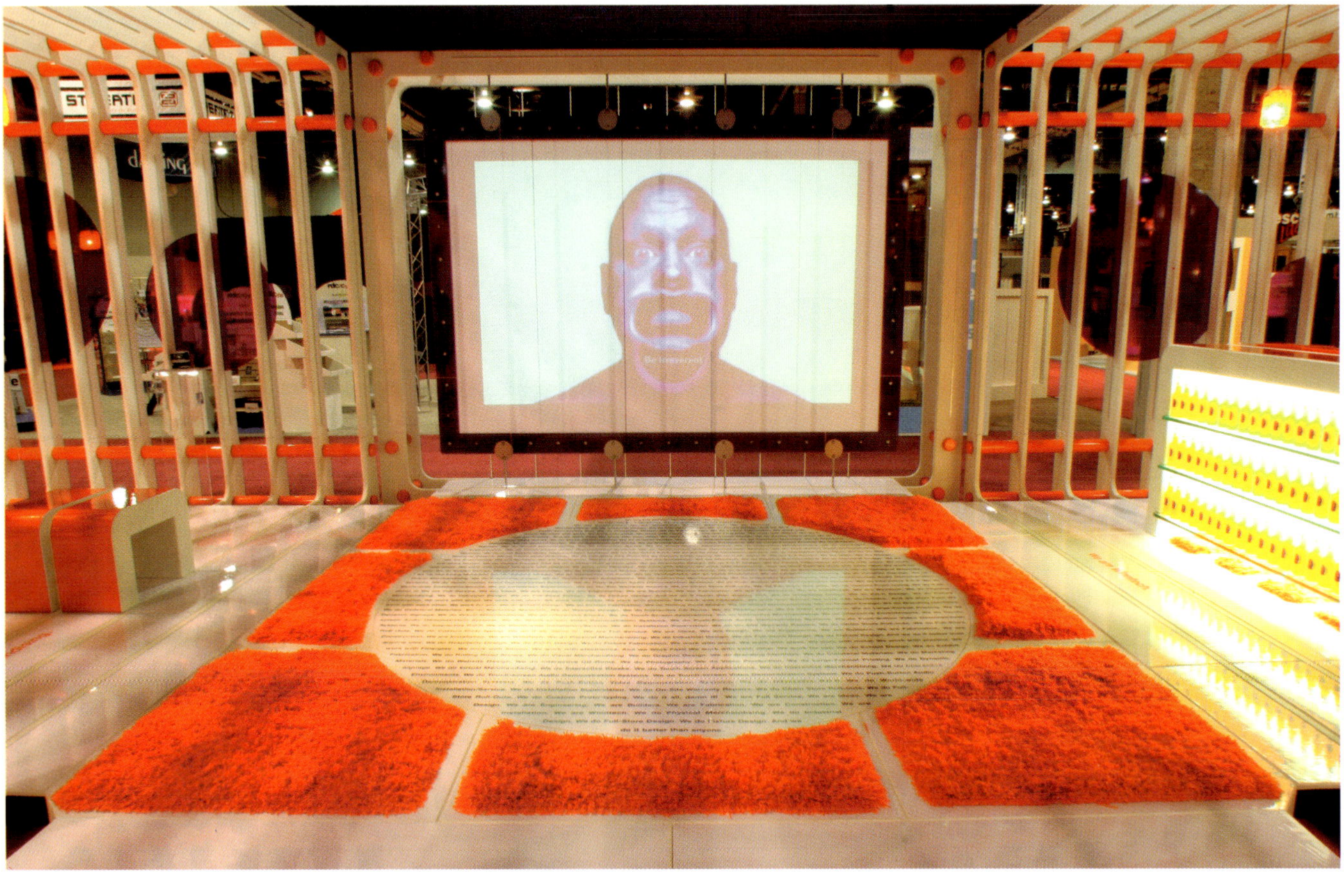

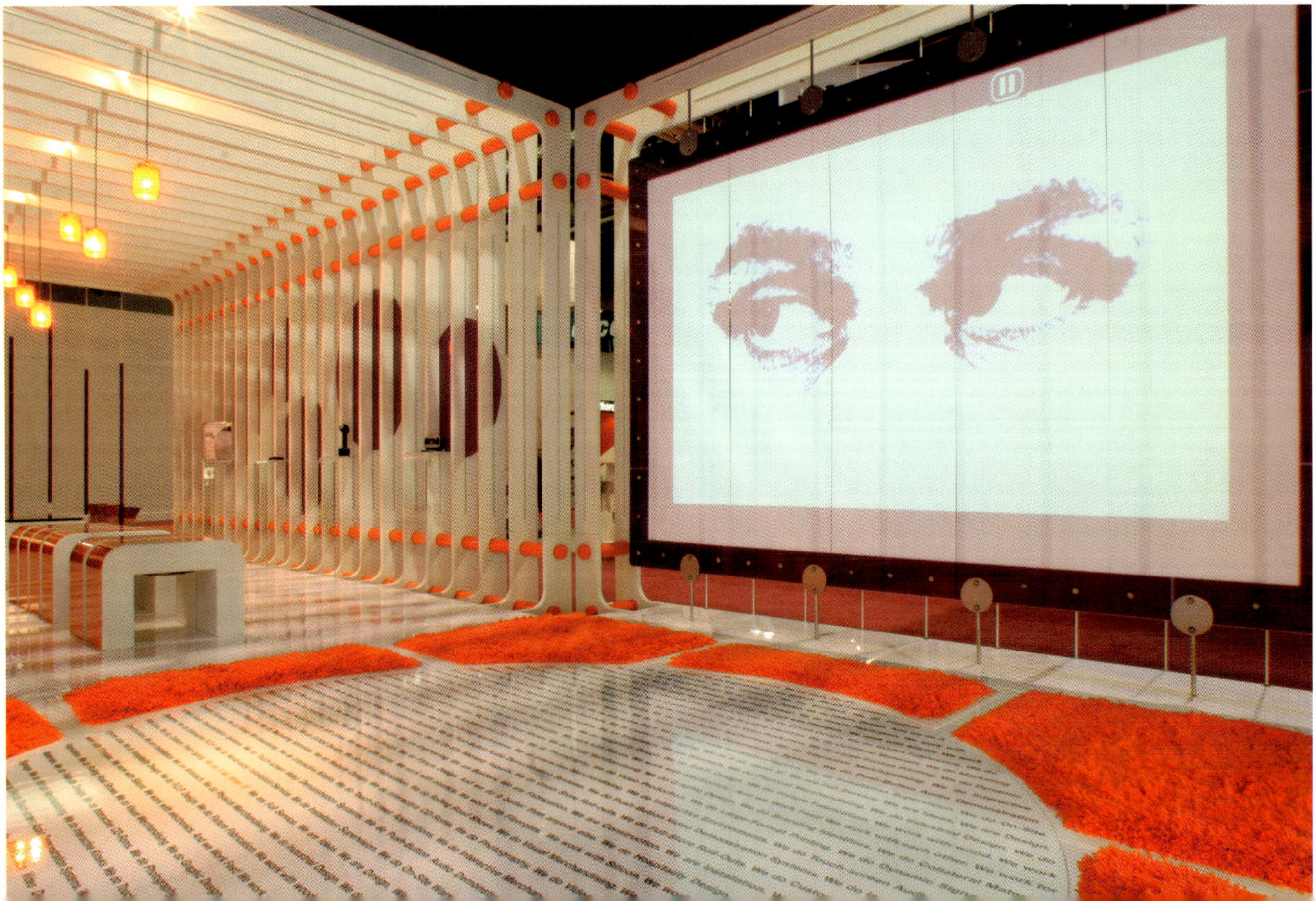

The cerise/purple disks recalled the Winntech logo and signature color and the logo graphic—in that color—appeared on a giant screen in the entry atrium where, on the floor, the designers repeated the very successful "carpet" filled with Winntech's attributes, abilities and services that had appeared in a much larger version in the 2004 exhibit. Surrounding the graphic circle were pieces of shag rug that highlighted and outlined the printed area rug. In addition, the lounge area was surrounded by individual product platforms that showed off a range of products designed by Winntech as merchandising solutions. Bottles of Clementine beverage—orange in color and flavor—were highlighted in the internally illuminated bar that was in the lounge area of the booth.

SAUCONY

1,500 SQUARE FEET

Flexible Modular Exhibit
Design: *Fitch:RPA, Powell, OH*
Creative Director: *David Denniston*
Sr. Environmental Designer: *Carrie Kenenth*
Project Manager: *Merilee Miller*
Communications Manager for Saucony:
    Austin Bishop
Fabrication: *Exhibitgroup/Giltspur, TX*
Photography: *Brandon King: Fitch:RPA*

70

Fitch:RPA was challenged by Saucony, an athletic shoe and apparel manufacturer, to create a flexible, modular exhibit stand that could fit into spaces as small as 20 ft. by 20 ft. or, when the space was available, open up to suit a 30 ft. by 50 ft. stand. The exhibit was scheduled to appear around the country at marathons and trade shows and thus—"adaptability and messaging were key." The design had to be able to "capture the essence of the advanced engineered running shoe in a consumer experience that emphasized the comradeship of the running community."

The "running experience" was enhanced in the exhibit by "arranging the furniture, fixtures and walls in a fluid layout that almost appears in motion—mimicking the smooth rhythm of running. These curves are juxtaposed with a rousing color palette—representing the charge a runner feels when training for a marathon."

The crisp colors, bright whites and the transparent details of the exhibit worked to overcome the "warehouse" feeling one often gets at a tradeshow. The circular lounge seating—the focal element—also is the heart of the space "created a multifunctional environment that allowed for its practical purpose of trying on shoes, while simultaneously facilitating a casual hangout and increased dwell time."

Modular 4 ft. wide panels were used to create the enclosure and on some of these panels, shoes were featured within half-round plastic domes. Along the curved back wall on the interior, shoes were displayed vertically as well as horizontally and forms, dressed in Saucony apparel, separated the shoe displays. More examples of the Saucony running shoes were seen "running" around the wood topped circular seating unit.

The designers integrated photo panels above the interior show displays that celebrated local marathon runners, "These panels invite the common runner into a shared understanding with the intent to make Saucony a part of their personal running community."

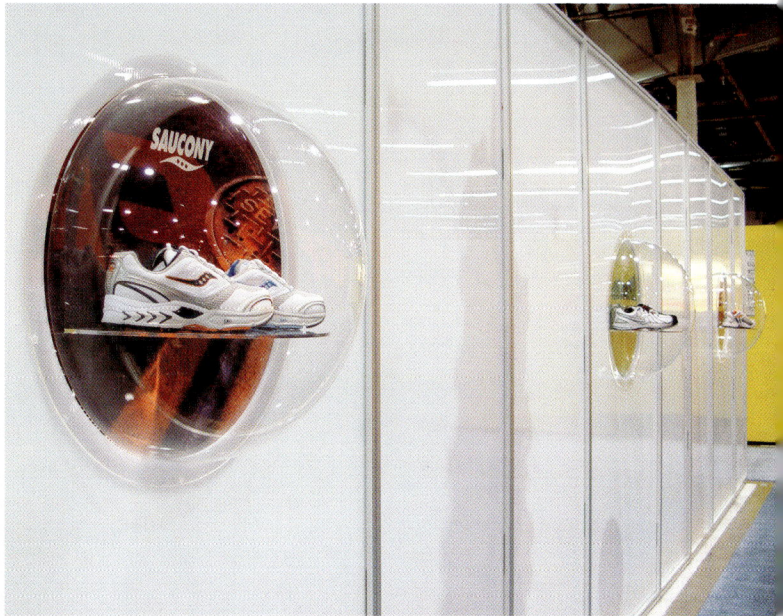

MAYTAG-JENNAIR

Kitchen & Bath Industry Show 2005,
     Las Vegas, NV
Design: *Phoenix Presentations*
Fabrication: *Phoenix Presentations & Transformit*
Photography: *Brett Drury*

The Maytag-JennAir company asked Phoenix Productions to come up with an eye-catching, image-building, product-selling setting for their 1,500 sq. ft. space at the Kitchen & Bath Industry Show in Las Vegas. As designed by Phoenix Presentations and realized in stretched fabric and wire framework by Transformit, the state-of-the-art appliances sat beneath softly curving fabric canopies. "This combination of style and substance is the perfect expression of the Maytag-JennAir brand."

The curling, waving and undulating "clouds" floated over the kitchen settings below. The metal framed forms—flushed with changing colors—were visible from a distance in the expo hall and brought visitors to this stand to see what was going on and what was being touted. These floating swirls were "a metaphor for steam and cooking aromas wafting over a kitchen." Not only did these airy elements attract attention, they also tended to lower the perceived ceiling height of the hall and thus affect a more residential feeling that was more in scale to the products on display in their lifestyle settings.

In addition to the product groupings, there were areas set aside for hospitality and conferencing. All these were connected visually by the many rings and bars of lighting equipment that projected the changing colors of light on to the "clouds." These provided not only color but "a feeling of warmth."

SINGAPORE TELECOMMUNICATIONS

1,550 SQUARE FEET

CommunicAsia 2005, Singapore
Design & Fabrication: *Pico Art International Pte, Ltd.*
Designers: *David Parkin & Tng Tang Li*
Product Manager: *Lee Lock Hong*
Account Servicing: *Pauline Tan*
Photography: *Pico Art International*

To promote SingTel (Singapore Telecommunications) at the CommunicAsia 2005 show in Singapore, David Parkin and Tng Tang Li, designers at Pico Art International, were able to add an oriental flavor to the contemporary design so that it "ideally represents SingTel as Asia's leading communications company."

To further reinforce the "BE" message that SingTel was telling in their 1,550 sq. ft. space, the lighted lantern cubes and the white fabric drapery were used. The exhibit space itself was like a soaring 20 ft.-plus cube of stretched fabric—illuminated from within—and on the exterior face, in addition to the SingTel name and logo, there were "BE" messages. Smaller cubes descended from the ceiling—surrounding the big cube—and in red-on-white and white-on-red repeated the same "BE" word.

The approximately 40 ft. by 40 ft. space was covered with a two-tier platform. Velour carpeting and laminates covered the platforms and there was an acrylic "trench"—filled with pebbles—that echoed the SingTel logo design. The on-the-floor demo counters were glowing light boxes and the bar counter was covered with lime green slate tiles. To enter the suspended giant cube that housed the reception area, guests had to step onto the "floating" second level platform. Inside, guests could see the advertising messages and images on illuminated cubes.

"The challenge for the production team was to align all the 'BE' messages on all the white fabric drapes smoothly and orderly in a straight manner."

LUNESTA

ACP, San Francisco, CA
Design: *Hamilton Exhibits, Indianapolis, IN Kevin Daugherty*
Photography: *Foster & Associates Photographers, Atlanta, GA*

1,600 SQUARE FEET

"When Sepracor, Inc. was planning to launch its new insomnia drug, Lunesta, one of their primary goals was to create a unique exhibit to enhance their brand in a manner unlike conventional exhibits. A great deal of work has been done on the branding including the creation of a luminescent butterfly icon. But they still were faced with the challenge of taking this theme from a concept to a trade show floor."

For the inner butterfly "wings" two, 20 ft. tall structures were designed "to convey the gossamer quality of a wing." The engineers were able to create a frame that was strong enough yet highly organic in look. This frame was covered in a translucent fabric. Attached to the outermost frame members were bundles of fiber optic rope lights. "The light system served to highlight the wings and edges and added to the surreal nature of the exhibit."

That is where Kevin Daugherty and Hamilton Exhibits of Indianapolis came in to create the floating, fluttering butterfly-like exhibit to fill the 1,600 sq. ft. space at the ACP show in San Francisco. Hamilton's design team translated the butterfly icon with gossamer fabrics, high resolution video images, subtle movement—and restful seating. The outer shell or cocoon was constructed by using structural tubing (provided by Optikenetics) that created a structure more like an aircraft wing than a trade show exhibit. Contained within this structure were fiber optic illuminators and over 60 miles of fiber optic cable. The individual wall panels were made of plywood and styrene. "On the inside of the cocoon walls a twinkling star-field gave the illusion of night."

To affect the opening and closing of the inner shell, the designers and engineers incorporated an 18 ft. Macton turntable with a carpeted plywood platform. One of the wing shapes was placed on the ground and the other attached to the lip of the platform. "When the turntable was activated the two wings moved from an overlapping condition to that of opposition—effectively enclosing the turntable in fabric wings." Ten chairs were grouped in the center of the turntable and attached to each was an HDTV video system from which they could watch "the show."

1,600 SQUARE FEET

Anaheim, CA
Design: *Lorenc + Yoo, Roswell, GA*
Fabrication: *MDM Scenery Works*
Graphic Fabrication: *Designer's Workshop*
Photography: *Rion Rizzo, Artistic Sources*

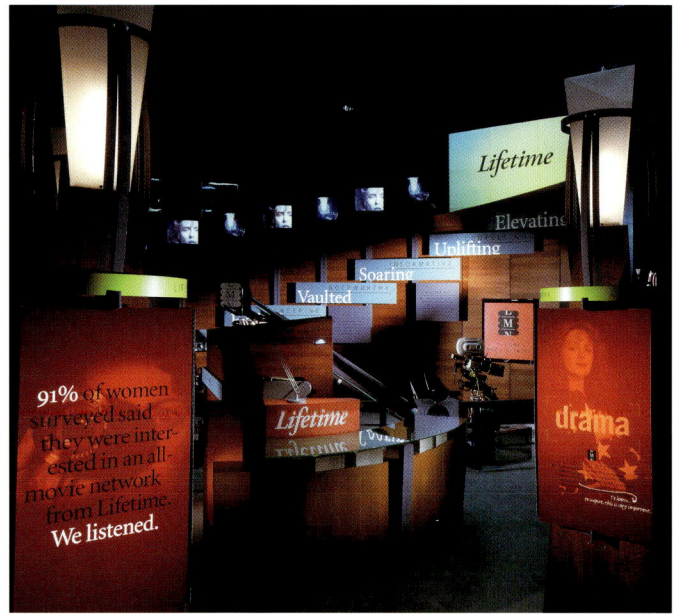

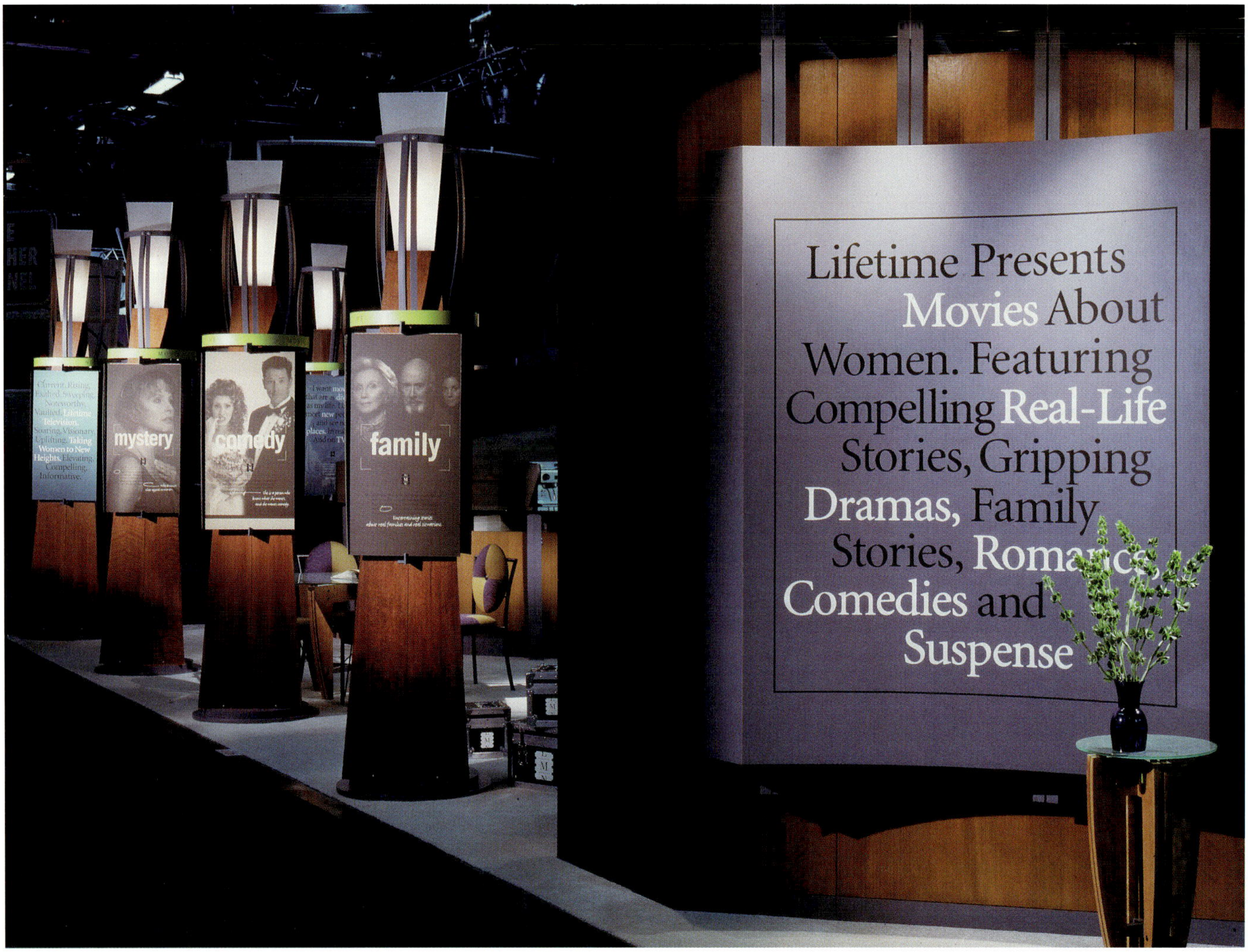

To launch Lifetime's Movie Channel, Lorenc + Yoo, a design firm in Roswell, GA, was invited to design an exhibit for a 1,600 sq. ft. space that would appeal to women aged 18 to 49. "In establishing a brand identity for the Lifetime Movie Network, we wanted to create a 'place' these women can turn to for films that motivate, inspire and move them."

Working with stage set builders and using materials atypical for an exhibit (wood veneers, painted metals and bold forms), the design was modularized so that it would be easy to ship, assemble and disassemble. The "bold forms" created an inviting, elegant and orderly environment within the mostly cluttered convention center floor. The colors were vibrant yet sophisticated.

One of the unique elements in the design was the installation of an actual movie boom crane and a panavision camera that lifted 14 ft. up in the air. It was used "to entice prospects with a bird's eye view of the trade show floor and the living room setting that was used as a background."

The corner location of the booth resembled a mini-studio complete with public and private areas with peep holes into both. An upswept, curving wall of cherry, mounted with messages and monitors, served as a backup for the crane and camera. On the other side of this wall were two semiprivate areas: a wedge shaped conference room bound by panels of translucent Plexiglas set in curved purple mullions, and an L-shaped honey oak fax/copy workroom.

In a corner was a mock-up of a living room set with a "hearth" and an entertainment center with a giant TV screen—and over 150 Lifetime movie cassettes. Along the two sides of the set there were seven poster obelisks displaying graphics. Crafted as tall triangles and topped with light lenses fastened by metal straps, they provided vibrant bright orange, blue-gray and green accents. A cappuccino stand with a boomerang shaped glass counter reflected the form of the feature wall behind the crane.

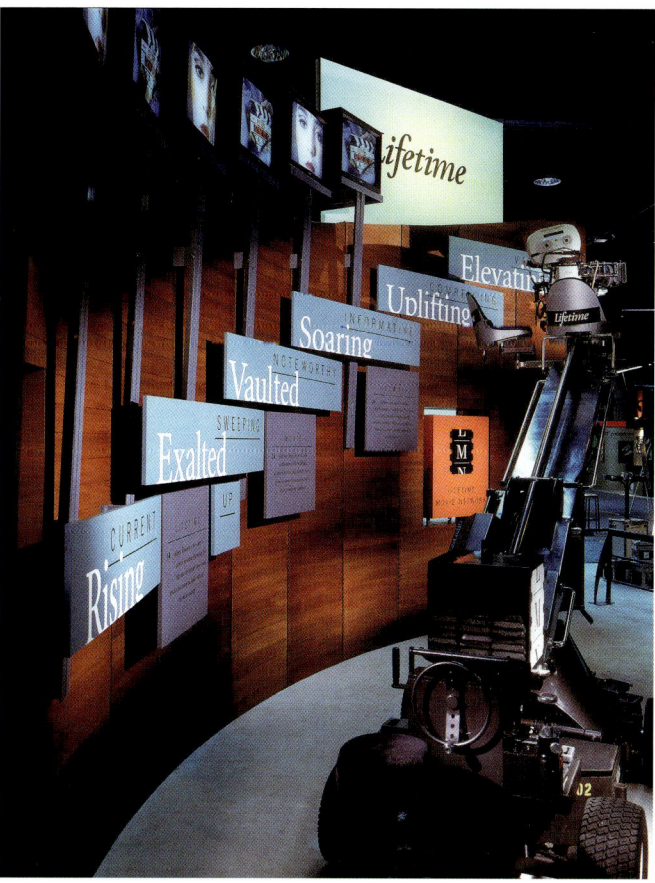

SIEMENS COMMUNICATIONS

2,000 SQUARE FEET

Networld Interop 2004, Las Vegas, NV
Design and Fabrication: *Exhibit Concepts*
Hanging Fabric Structures and Kiosk: *Moss, Inc.*
Photography: *Courtesy of Exhibit Concepts*

80

Exhibit Concepts designed and fabricated this "rental package" for Siemens Communications to use at six trade shows over a two year period. Since the exhibit spaces varied from 3,600 sq. ft. to 2,000 sq. ft. down to 1,600 sq. ft., all the elements were modular and adaptable and could be reconfigured to suit the particular space.

The exhibit's focus was to allow one-on-one interaction with attendees on a variety of networking opportunities offered by the Siemens Enterprise and Carrier divisions. "It was critical to elevate Siemens' brand and to incorporate visual continuity in the graphics." Moss, Inc. was called upon to produce the backlit, stretched fabric plumes on aluminum frames that accentuated the workstations on the floor as well as the overhanging graphic panels. These, too, were produced with stretch fabric over lightweight aluminum frames. These sweeps and swoops and visually animated forms provided a feeling of action and lightness to the wood-like laminate finishes on the interactive stations clustered on the multicolored carpeted floor.

The color palette featured the cool blues of the stretched fabric forms, the carpet patterned in yellow, gray and blue and the warm-toned mainly orange and red graphic panels. For some of the trade shows the designers incorporated a "theater" with a home kitchen and an office work space to demonstrate Siemens services and products.

The exhibit debuted at Networld Interop 2004 in Las Vegas where it received a "Best in Show" award.

CAMBRIA

2,000 SQUARE FEET

Kitchen & Bath Industry Show 2005,
Las Vegas, NV
Design & Construction: *Parallel*
Designer: *Shawn King*
Strategist: *Lisa Cook*
Photography: *Steve Smith, edge 5*

Cambria produces quartz surfaces for countertops, vanities, flooring, etc. in many beautiful colors. The quartz is also strong and has carefree durability. What Cambria wanted from nParallel, a brand communications/merchandising strategy and display agency, was an exhibit for the 2,000 sq. ft. space that would "capture retailers, architects and builders, designers and consumers, and engage them in the experience of the Cambria brand."

The design, created and constructed by nParallel for the Kitchen & Bath Industry show in Las Vegas, was rooted in classical Georgian architecture. A curving, lighted trellis along the front of the booth framed and supported the "museum quality display" of quartz surfaces. 2 ft. by 2 ft. and 2 ft. by 6 ft. slabs of quartz were shown on the 4 ft. wide by 12 ft. tall wall panels so that they were readily visible in the expo hall even from a distance. The space between the trellised display wall units made the colors visible from all angles around the booth and established an open view to the interior and thus invited visitors to enter.

Lighting and color contributed to the overall impact of the booth's design. The black of the interior walls and the overhead Cambria sign created a neutral backdrop for the colors of the samples of quartz and allowed them to stand out. "The effect suggested the experience of theater—from the darkness the colors came to light and life."

One of the major problems facing the designers was the weight of the slabs. Since each 2 ft. by 2 ft. slab weighed in at 100 pounds, the weight had to be supported safely without the supporting structure appearing dominant or overpowering the entire design. By using powder coated steel and a classic black and white scheme nParallel was able to meet the challenge.

KOHLER

Bathroom Expo, Excel, UK
Design: *Checkland Kindleysides, London, UK*
Photography: *Adrian Wilson*

The Kohler brand of bathroom fixtures was launched at the Bathroom Expo in Excel, UK in a 2,200 sq. ft. space. As designed by Checkland Kindleysides of London, who has in the past designed Kohler showrooms, the stand featured working product displays,

A basin from each of Kohler's style ranges was presented along the outside of the enclosed exhibit space. On the interior, however, the display showed units from each range or design line in more innovative ways—

Design, style & innovation

Design at its best enriches our lives,
allowing us to find pleasure
in the things that surround us

Across the broadest range of bathroom products
the KOHLER® commitment to design and
visual integrity is uncompromising.

"communicating the core values and personality of the brand via more abstract 'art' displays, depicting key aspects of the products and introducing visitors to the 'experience of bathing' with Kohler." A series of 12 ft. tall panels with oversized graphics on top served as backups for the wash basins displayed on the façade. The spaces between these panels opened into the interior space of the stand and allowed easy access for visitors. The backs of these partitions—the side facing inside the space—supported artistic arrangements of products such as basins, faucets and other appliances presented as decorative art pieces. Behind one of these façade panels was a spouting "fountain" with numerous streams of water flowing into a black basin. On the wall was inscribed "Design, Style and Innovation." Another message in the booth read, "Design at its best enriches our lives allowing us to find pleasure in the things that surround us."

To bring home that point and point up how the various Kohler products can "enrich our surroundings," the exhibit was highlighted with a series of model bathrooms designed by some of England's top interior designers.

87

HANAROTELECOM

2,280 SQUARE FEET

ITU Telecom Asia 2004, Busan, South Korea
Design & Construction: *Kingsmen Korea*
Photography: *Noon Pictures*

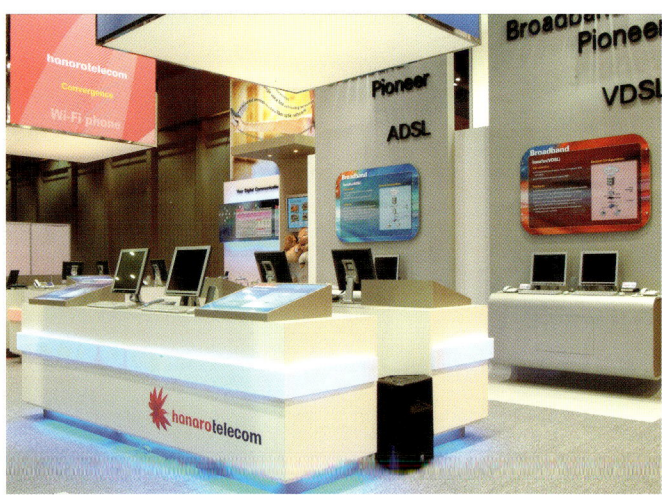

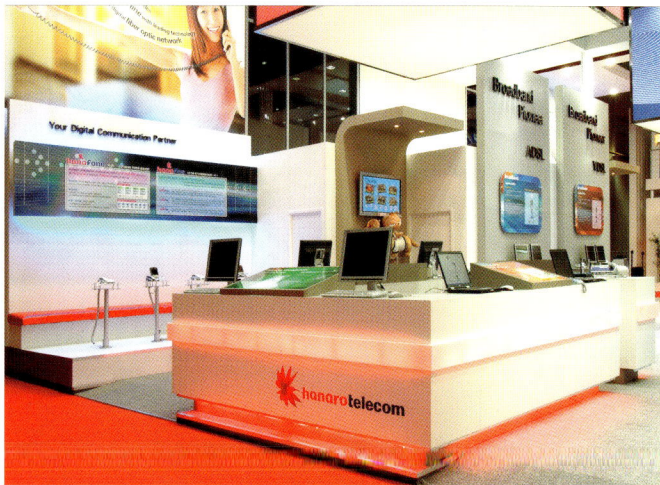

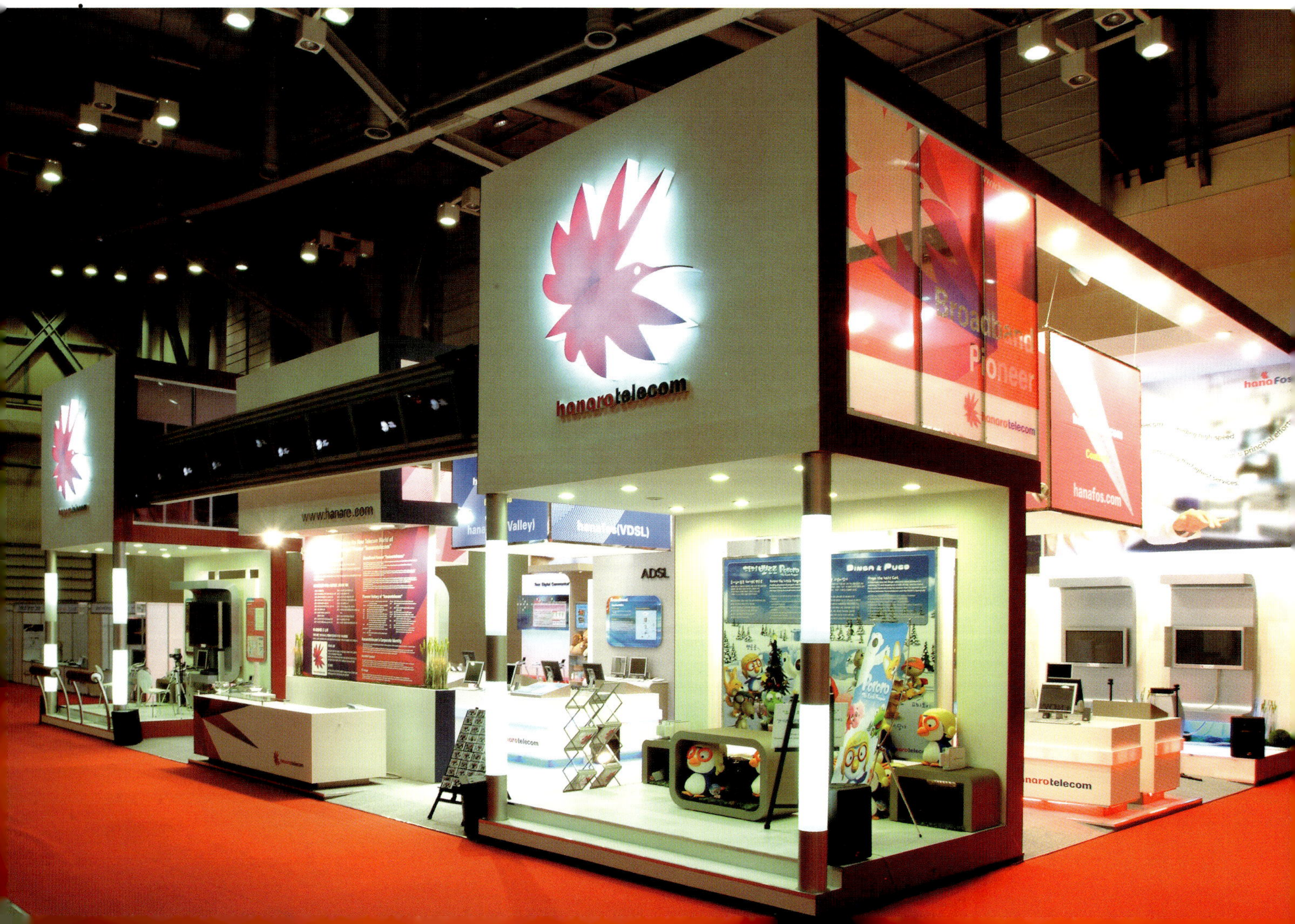

Hanarotelecom is a pioneer in broadband services in South Korea and to present their new corporate identity at the ITU Telecom Asia show in Busan, South Korea, they had Kingsmen's Korean subsidiary design their 2,280 sq. ft. stand.

The "new corporate identity" was one that suggested "a young and enterprising spirit." Because they were on a tight schedule, the designers came up with this single-story structure that was eye-catching and "significantly reflected hanarotelecom's corporate identity." To suggest "continuity," the company's corporate colors were used to highlight and accentuate the edges of the main structure. "This in turn represented hanarotelecom's continuous search for innovation in digital communication." The predominantly white exhibit was composed of several 16 ft. tall panels with 8 ft. wide spaces between them and they enclosed the central exhibit area but still left spacious openings through which visitors could freely enter. Over the information desk, in the front opening of

the stand, there was a bridge of TV monitors that added a sense of movement and excitement to the action below. The interior space was furnished with interactive testing stations where the attendees could actually sample the company's newest products and services. Suspended overhead were fabric-covered, illuminated cubes that served to highlight some of the demo stations on the floor.

The crisp, clean design and the projection of the company's logo colors helped to "further the company's commitment to creating a world of convenience through digital communication."

TEKNION

IIDEX International Interior Design Expo,
Toronto, ON
Design: *Burdifilek, Toronto, ON*

2,400 SQUARE FEET

Burdifilek, the Toronto based design firm, was able to "create an unconventional corporate environment" with the exhibit they designed for Teknion that appeared at the IIDEX show in Toronto. For the 2,400 sq. ft. space they "incorporated a sense of high fashion into a typical 'office lifestyle' while highlighting the company's new European themed office line." The result won them a "Best of Canada" award.

The stand reeks of drama and sophistication. The design team used classic modernist forms combined with unexpected materials and finishes. There was sleek, high gloss black teamed with flesh-toned glass under a lilac to skin-toned gradated ceiling. The wool carpet beneath was also flesh-toned and imported black silk fringe appeared all through the design. The long fringe insured a sense of privacy but did not impede entrance into the booth structure that was conceived as "a private showroom" on the expo floor.

The ceiling system and lighting were a single floating component—independent of the walls of the exhibit. The structure, itself, was designed with modular parts with internal seams that disguised the joints. That permitted off-site manufacture and finishing and easy on-site installation. Lucite wall panels and the fringe curtains were also detailed to fit into a slot system that would allow for height adjustments. Everything was designed by Burdifilek to "minimalize the installation period."

"Teknion's new furniture system debuted in black, white and lilac—unconventional and striking against a warm and expressive booth design. The overall concept represented Teknion's dedication to creativity and became a signature example of temporary architecture."

SYNOPSYS

Design Automation Conference 2005,
         Anaheim, CA
Design and Fabrication: *Exhibitgroup/Giltspur*
Fabric Component: *Transformit*
Photography: *Courtesy of Exhibitgroup/Giltspur*

2,400 SQUARE FEET

It was almost impossible to miss the bright, strong colored curls of fabric stretched over aluminum frames that soared over the 2,400 sq. ft. space occupied by Synopsys at the Design Automation Conference in Anaheim, CA. The sweeping, curling forms were "a 3D experiential representation of the Synopsys brand." Where usually these fabric forms depend upon colored light to animate them, for this occasion the fabrics were dyed these strong, attracting colors.

A giant rolling wave of purple fabric started out near the entrance to the space and swept back past the upright fabric walls that were also curled and swirled. A half round information desk appeared right off the major traffic aisle and to one side were conference tables with bright blue chairs. Plasma screens, atop black pedestals, served each "conference" cluster. The dense black flooring delineated Synopsys' space and also sharply contrasted with the white and silvery metal work/demo stations on the floor and the partitions that were capped with the rich purple color of the company's logo. Set back in the space—under a semicircle of purple stretched fabric emblazoned with the Synopsys logo sat a silvery information desk: the nerve center of the booth's design.

95

MIZUNO

2,535 SQUARE FEET

4th China Beijing International Golf Expo 2005, Beijing, China
Exhibit Design & Fabrication: *Shanghai Pico Exhibition Services Co., Ltd. China*
Designer: *Max Liu*
Photography: *Courtesy of Pico Shanghai*

Mizuno is a manufacturer of golf equipment and for their appearance at the 4th China International Golf Expo in the China World Trade Center in Beijing, China, the firm wanted to not only promote its brand image to the golfing industry but "contribute to society through the advancement of sports and quality sporting goods."

The front of the booth consisted of white fins that reached up from the ceiling of the first level of this two story structure to semi-reveal a giant wall graphic and the second level's conferencing area. The same fin arrangement, with plasma screens overlaid, appeared at ground

level—in the middle of the booth—to effectively divide and provide two spacious entrances into the space. As designed by Max Liu of Pico Shanghai, the 2,535 sq. ft. space suggested—in form—the arch shape of a golf club. Mizuno's signature blue color appeared throughout the space to "create a cool blue environment and an over-all atmosphere of excitement and motion." Black and white with bold shots of red were used in the showroom areas of the exhibit—the ground level. The rear wall was framed with square arches of black that surrounded fields of white upon which the Mizuno products were displayed. The angled, rectangular framed floor units carried through the same design feeling and they, too, were accented with red striping. The white floor carpet "also created a feeling of big and open space." The entire ground level was brightly illuminated with incandescent spots recessed into the dropped ceiling as well as located within the frames that surrounded the wall mounted products.

The second level served as a spacious meeting area enhanced by the large product posters "where visitors could experience the spirit of golf activity."

Mizuno's management was pleased with the results of the show booth and they were also proud to have their space recognized as the "Best Concept" for the 2005 Beijing Golf Expo.

PANASONIC

2,800 SQUARE FEET

CommunicAsia 2005, Singapore
Exhibit Design & Fabrication: *Pico Art*
      International Pte Ltd., Singapore
Design: *David Parkin & Krystal Liau*
Photography: *Courtesy of Pico Art International*

Visible from anywhere in the CommunicAsia expo hall in Singapore was the gigantic illuminated fabric covered ceiling that soared over Panasonic's 2,800 sq. ft. space. Though all the action was centered on the interactive units/demo stations and the exhibition areas on the raised white floor, it was the striking white ceiling accented with Panasonic's logo blue on all four sides that held together all the action below. The ceiling was designed with numerous rectangular shapes that angled along the four sides and ceiling contained many lamps that brightly illuminated the exhibit below.

Most of the floor space was open so that attendees in the surrounding aisles could readily step up and into —and get involved with any of the many black or white demo stations and exhibits. One corner of the space was totally blocked off and here the black exterior surface served to accentuate the strong, backlit graphic panels set into it. On the inner side of this corner construction there was a series of areas devoted to the various Panasonic products—away from the tumult on the floor. On the glass enclosed mezzanine of this built-up area—directly under the light-box ceiling was a space where live entertainment, mainly dance, was performed.

For this exhibit a special software program was developed and it was incorporated into the stations on the floor. "Holopoint" was a jigsaw puzzle type game where people who solved parts of the puzzle could advance to the next stop—and so on—till a Jackpot winner was declared. This helped draw crowds to the exhibit space.

LUCENT TECHNOLOGIES

3,170 SQUARE FEET

Design & Fabrication: *Pico Art International Pte Ltd.*
Designer: *Yvette Lim Bee Leng*
Creative Director: *Azmi Tarmuji*
Graphic Designer: *Mohd Yazid*
Technical Head: *Kevin Kong*
Photography: *Courtesy of Pico Art International*

The two story high exhibit for Lucent Technologies, designed by Pico Art, appeared in a 3,170 sq. ft. space at CommunicAsia 2005 in Singapore. Throughout the space the design team used elements of transparency and translucency to create a light, open and spacious environment that would complement ,and be complemented by, the special lighting effects.

Suspended from the framed, lamp-filled rectangular ceiling that hovered over the floor was fabric stretched over metal frames forms that carried the Lucent Technologies logo as well as the company's messages. These tubular "lampshades" were illuminated in assorted colors. "Translucent colored fabric lit with colored moving special lighting effects provided a dynamic and attractive visual treat while adding dazzling effects to the stand."

Spread out throughout the floor of the stand were clusters of demonstration pods that invited attendees to try out the new products and technologies. These units were modular in design so that they could be arranged or rearranged as needed. Panels of multi-striped material appeared in the space and highlighted the bar and the information desk that was located in a prominent corner. The company's signature red color was used for a sharp accent note and also appeared on focal walls. One of them was the bold two story high red wall with a super-graphic on top accentuated the staircase that led visitors up to the V.I.P area above the hubbub of the expo floor. Here there were "lush red sofas, velvety carpet flooring, warm lighting—a plush and perfect setting in which to entertain clients."

Overall, the space had "a corporate and professional look" that was also inviting, educational 3,600 square feet.

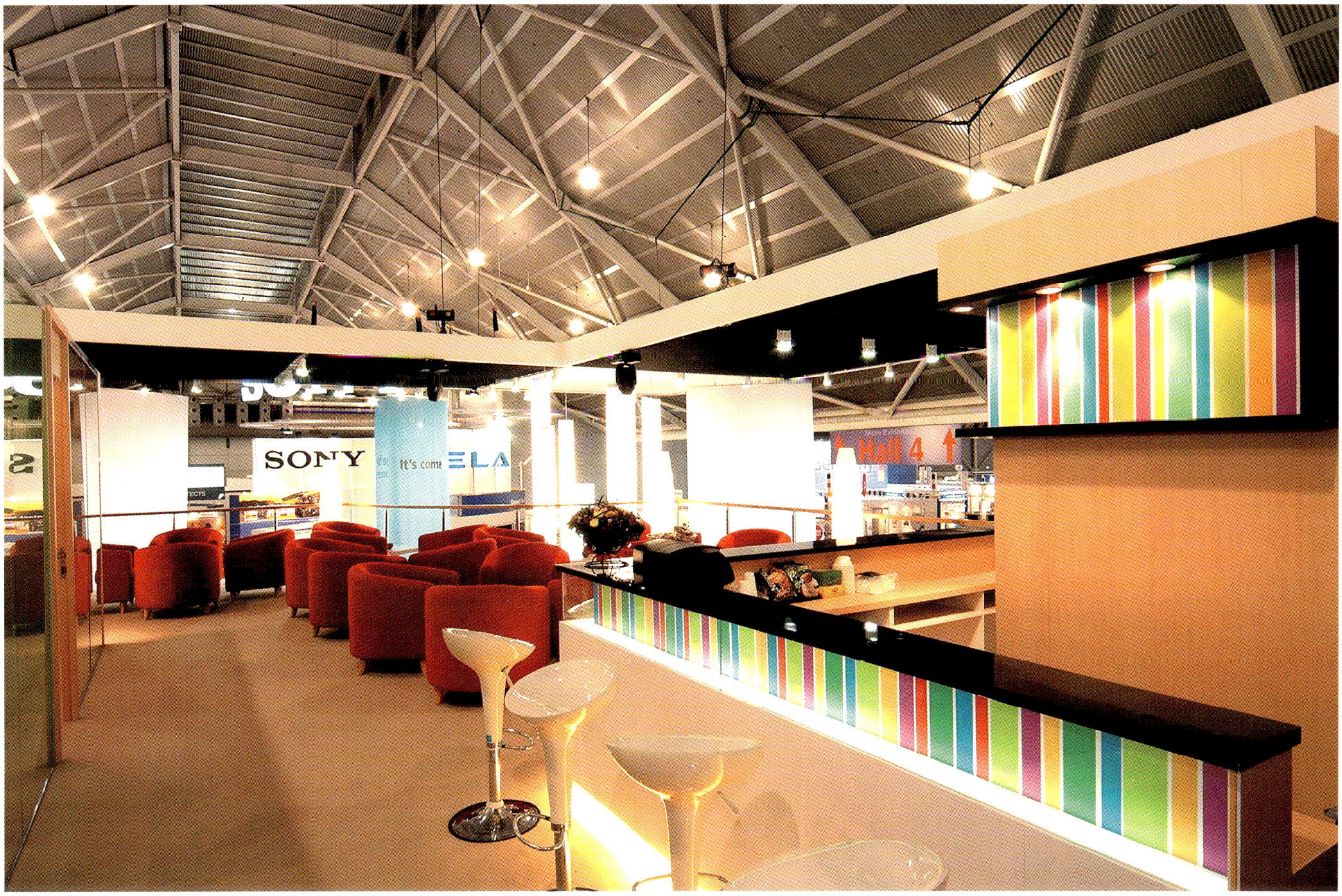
SONY
Hall 4

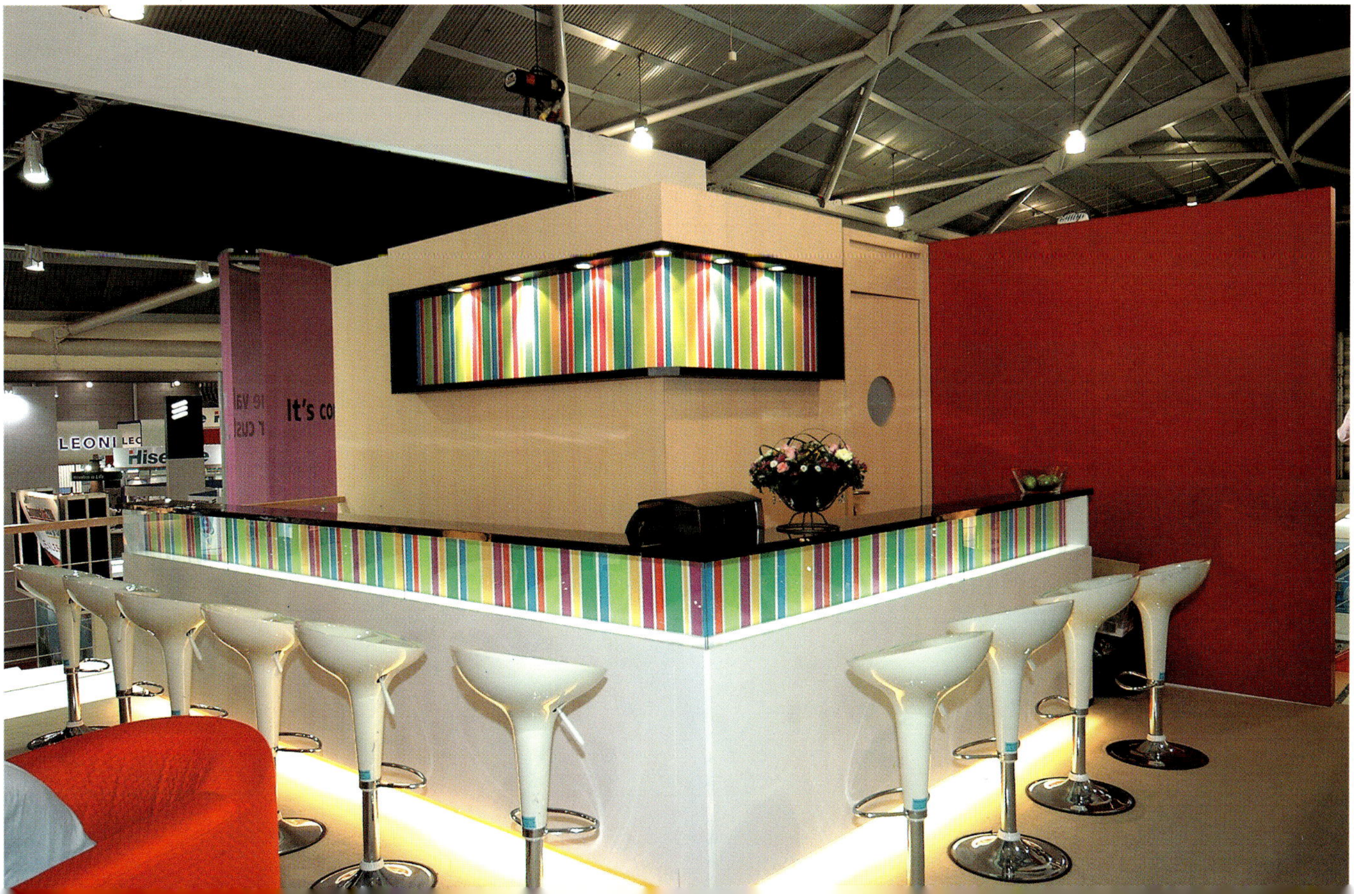
LEONI

MICROSOFT — GAMES FOR WINDOWS

E3: Electronic Entertainment Expo, 2005,
    Los Angeles, CA
Design & Fabrication: *Pinnacle Exhibits*
Photography: *Guy Lewis*

E3 is all about entertainment! It is about games, TV, movies and any and all forms of having electronic fun. Microsoft took a 3,600 sq. ft. space at the recent show in Los Angeles to present their Games for Windows to a horde of entertainment seeking visitors.

?,??? SQUARE FEET

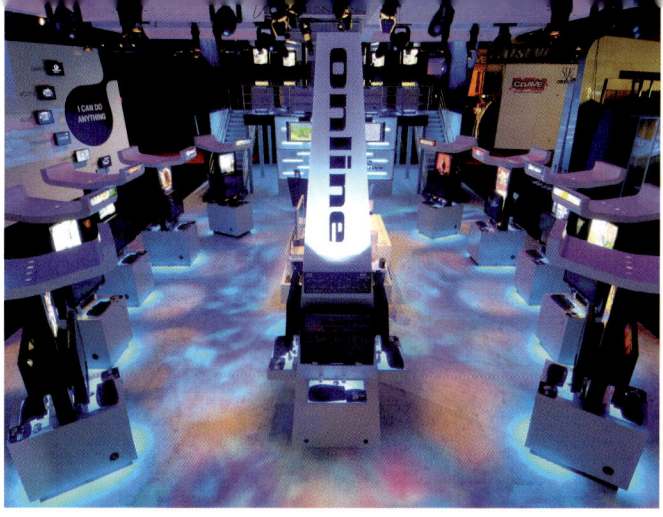

In the space, as designed by Pinnacle Exhibits, there was easy access and lots of free space for movement with myriad opportunities for the visitors to interact with—or play with—the new products. Here Microsoft was able to promote their Games for Windows as a "hip, cool gaming platform." The large central zone or hub of the exhibit contained about a dozen stations where two or more gamesters could sample the new programs and/or games. This area was accentuated by six gigantic rectangular blocks of fabric-covered metal frames that were suspended from the expo hall's ceiling. Light induced patterns of color "played" on and off these units. Blue lighting predominated throughout most of the exhibit space and was used "as a nod to Microsoft" and also as a background for the real color: the many colors that came from the oversized demonstration monitors.

According to the design team, "The exhibit structure was kept simple and there were no large game graphics or character cutouts. This enabled the games themselves to be the big 'wow!' within the environment." The large, high resolution monitors highlighted the superiority of the games' graphics. The Microsoft logo was purposefully kept to a minimum and ranked below the game title in the graphics hierarchy.

This central interactive core of the space was contained by two multistory structures that boasted of meeting rooms, hospitality areas and storage space. Stairs led to the upper stories and the constructions were mainly translucent panels within a modular grid framework. The overall look of the exhibit emphasized that "the games for this platform are far more sophisticated and have better graphics than their gaming console counterparts."

QATAR PETROLEUM

3.700 SQUARE FEET

Doha International Expo Center, Doha, UAE
Exhibit Design & Fabrication: *Pico Dubai International L.L.C.*
Designer: *Ricardo Angeles*
Account Executive: *Stanley Norris*
In Charge of Production: *Pradeep Kumar*
Photography: *Courtesy of Pico Dubai*

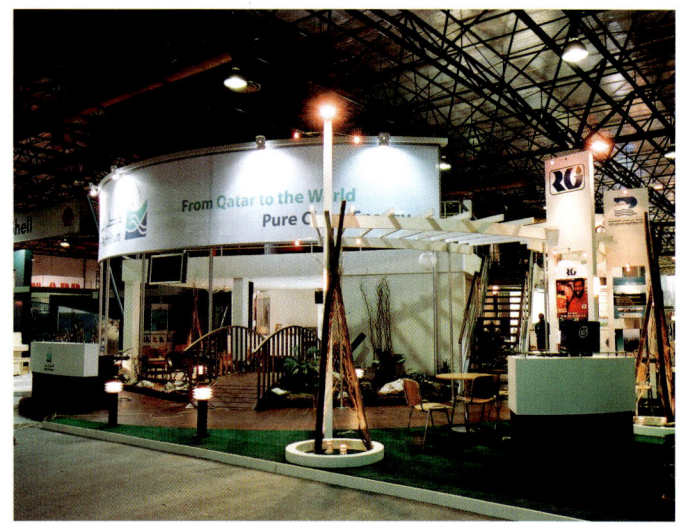

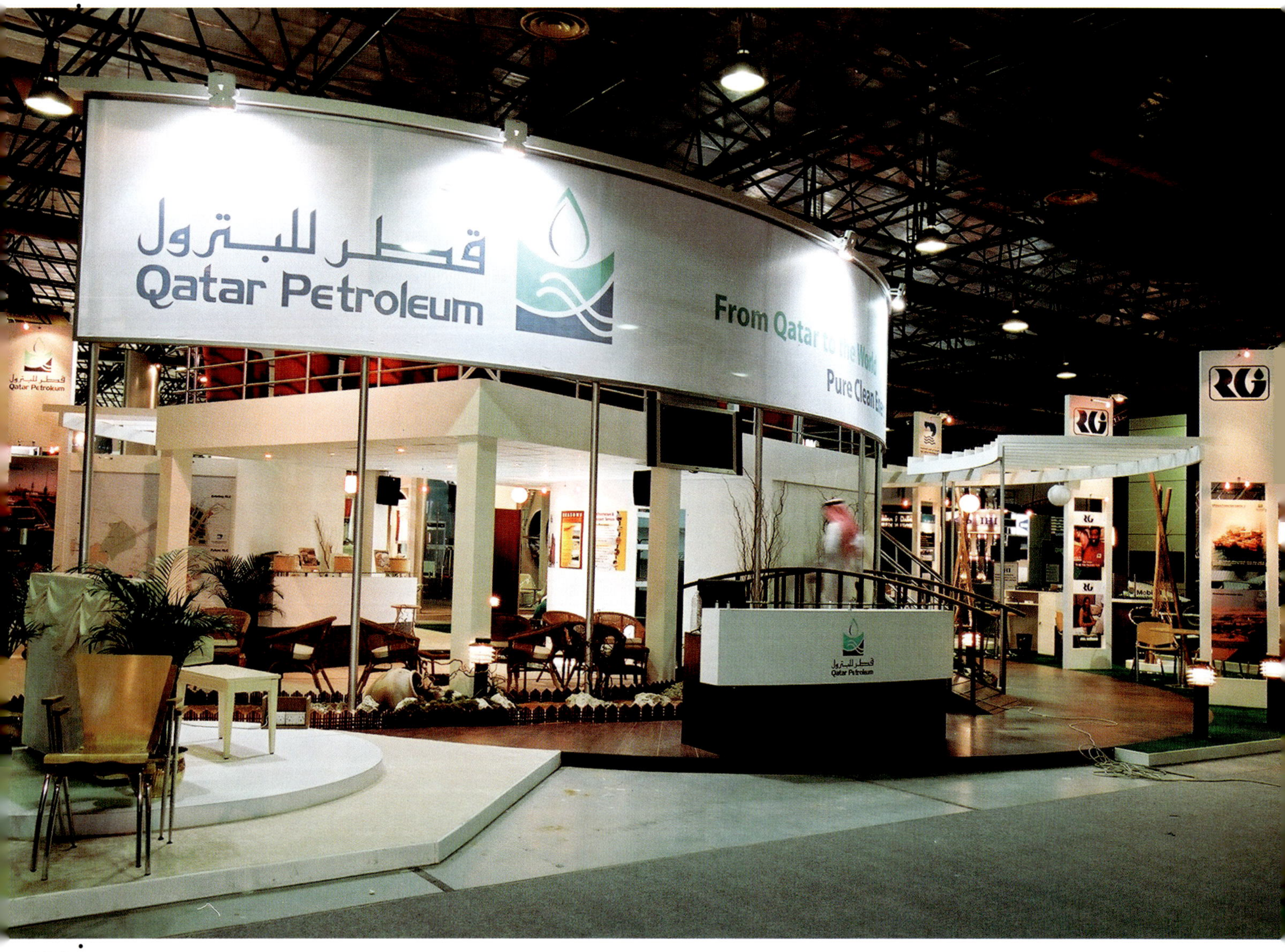

The theme developed by Pico Dubai for Qatar Petroleum was "Nature and Gardens." Since Qatar Petroleum supports and is actively involved in ecological balance and matters of the earth's atmosphere—it seemed like a match.

To bring the essence of "nature" to the 3,700 sq. ft. stand in Doha's International Expo Center's hall, the designers selected wood and astro-turf grass mats to cover the floor and trellises that added to the "garden" ambiance. There was also a landscaped wadi and adding to the tropical atmosphere were the bamboo theme pylons that were erected along the outer boundaries of the stand.

From a distance visitors could see the "message" from the oil company stretched across in a sweeping arc of fabric over a metal frame. Once they were closer, attendees were welcomed into the garden-like space and invited to enjoy the relaxing music being played by a pianist. A bridge connected the lounge area to the refreshment bar and to further the relaxed, outdoor attitude of the design, a mini golf course was constructed where guests could putter or play. For presentations, a special zone equipped with a large plasma screen was erected at the rear of the space.

V.I.P. guests and clients were invited to partake of the hospitality and conferencing zones set up on the mezzanine which was partially screened off from the expo hall by the semicircular fabric framed swath of signage previously mentioned.

MOTOROLA

3,700 SQUARE FEET

CommunicAsia 2005, Singapore
Design & Fabrication: *Pico Art International Pte Ltd.*
Design Director: *Azmi Bin Tarmuji*
Account Manager: *Jack Chia*
Photography: *Courtesy of Pico Art International*

Three upward sweeping "walls"—almost 23 ft. tall—reached up to support the gigantic ring that seemed to float over the 3,700 sq. ft. Motorola exhibit space at CommunicAsia 2005 in Singapore. The black ring supported the Motorola name and logo—in blue and yellow—and made the booth instantly viewable from anywhere in the hall. It also served to carry most of the theatrical lighting that was used to produce the colorful and kinetic effects on the floor.

As designed and constructed by Pico Art, the central unit was constructed of laminated timber and finished in black. The rich deep color was offset by the internally-illuminated logo and by the vibrant violet colored flooring. Each of the three rising elements started from a black circular pod which was equipped with interactive stations highlighted in yellow and metallic silver.

These circular platforms were stepped up off the carpet and hidden lights created red haloes around reach station/pod.

A catwalk platform with a projection screen was centered in the stand and the circle motif introduced in the pods was echoed throughout the space in the open, round booths that were accentuated by "Here" signage. According to the design team, there were several of these experiential sectors created such as "Here Music," "Here Drink," and "Here Make-Up." In these zones attendees could relax while sampling Motorola products and the company's hospitality and "thus deepen the consumer's relationship." The brand was furthered by the "experience" provided in the exhibit stand rather than by simple logo projection alone.

4,880 SQUARE FEET

SVIAZ/ EXPO Center 2005, Moscow, Russia
Design: *Lorenc + Yoo, Roswell, GA*
Fabrication & Collaborator: *GL Associates, Seoul, South Korea*
Photography: *Courtesy of GL Associates*

The space occupied by Samsung Telecommunications Network at the SVIAZ Moscow Show consisted of two adjacent spaces.

The larger one, 40 ft. by 80 ft. was dedicated to product displays and demonstrations. The smaller one, 42 ft. by 40 ft., was used for network system equipment display, meetings and media rooms.

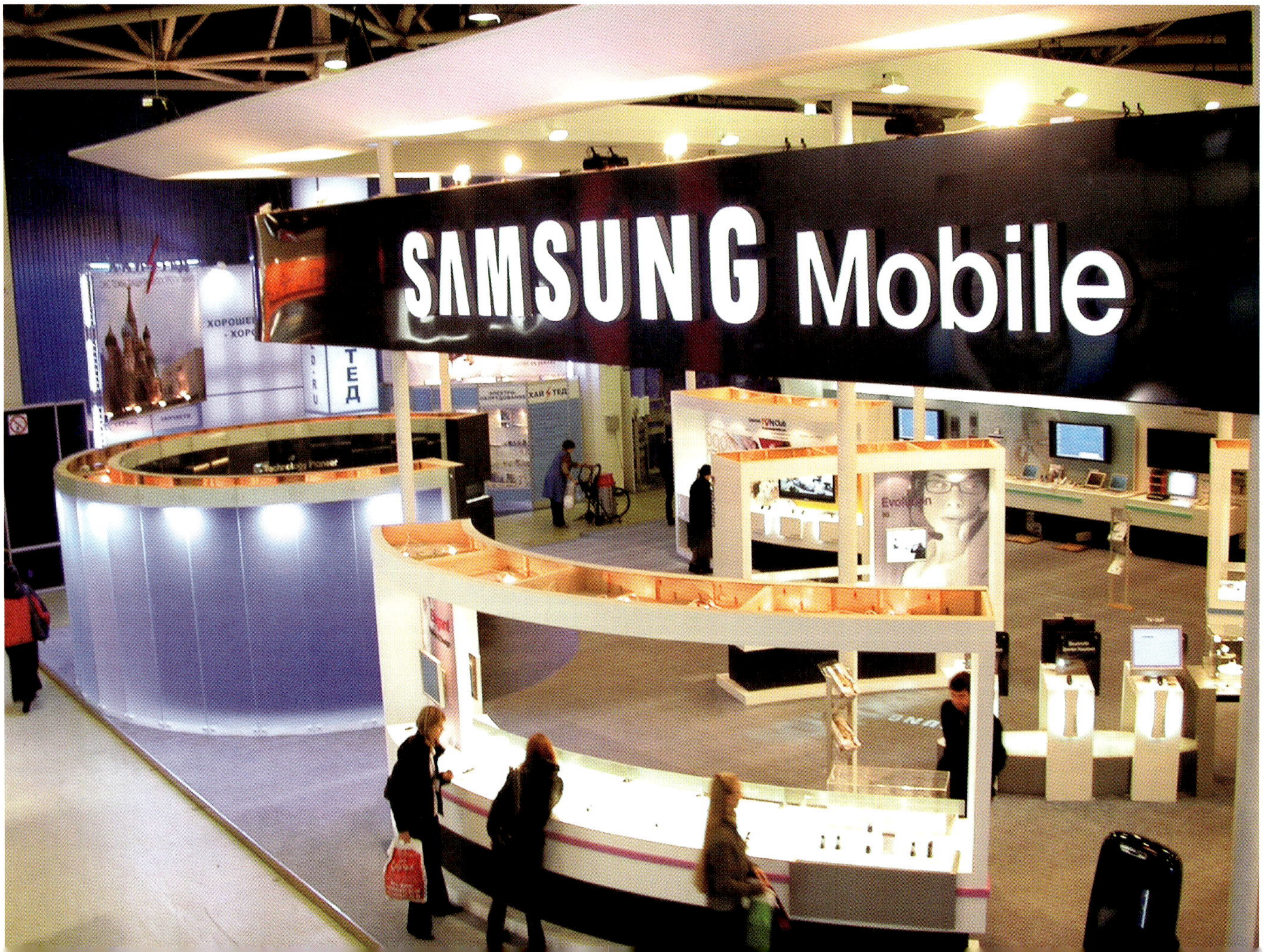

Lorenc + Yoo of Roswell, GA worked with GL Associates of Seoul to "create a unified exhibit identity for regional telecommunication-related shows in Asia." The new design provided that every person who comes into contact

with a Samsung TN booth at any exhibition or trade show would have "a strong, clear and consistent image of the brand." The plan called for locating key products along the distant edge of the space and thus allow visitors to enter through the main aisle. This served to offer some closure from the adjacent booths. There was minimal enclosure for the larger display area to ensure an easy traffic flow and the main reception desk was anchored in the front corner and visible from both aisles. This main exhibit area was divided into four zones: Evolution, Exciting, Efficient and Elegant.

The zones were designed to appear as though they were on two levels covered by a large ceiling and an overhead sign. "The ground plane had transparency into the space, allowing room for viewing the products." At the approach to the exhibit there was a blue, glazed, circular wall called

"the Gallery." The high-end products were showcased here and at the opposite end was Samsung Fun Club—a more action-oriented space.

The internal promotional graphics were kept in controlled areas "so that they did not create visual clutter." To keep the space "contemporary and airy" the color palette was predominantly white, black along with the signature blue and silver.

Exciting
Mobile Theater
Efficient

Exciting
Evolution

ХАЙТЕД
СИСТЕМЫ ЗАЩИТЫ ЭЛЕКТРОПИТАНИЯ
Technology Pioneer
THE GALLERY

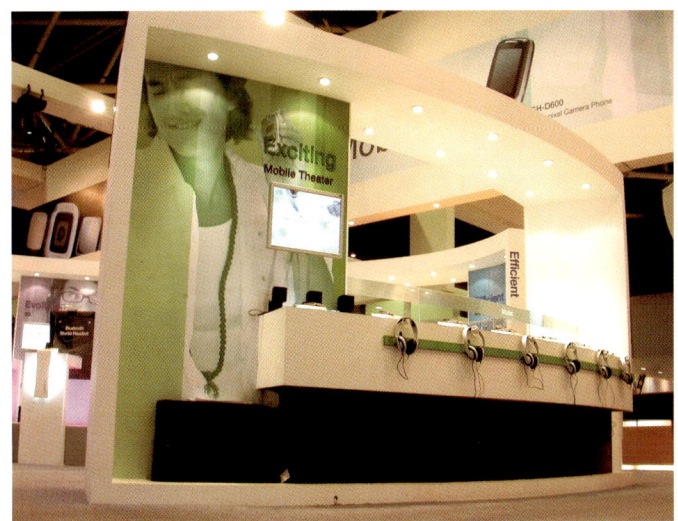

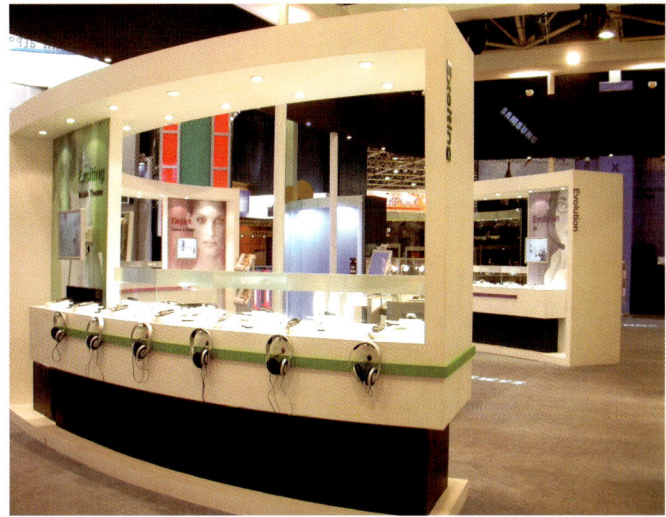

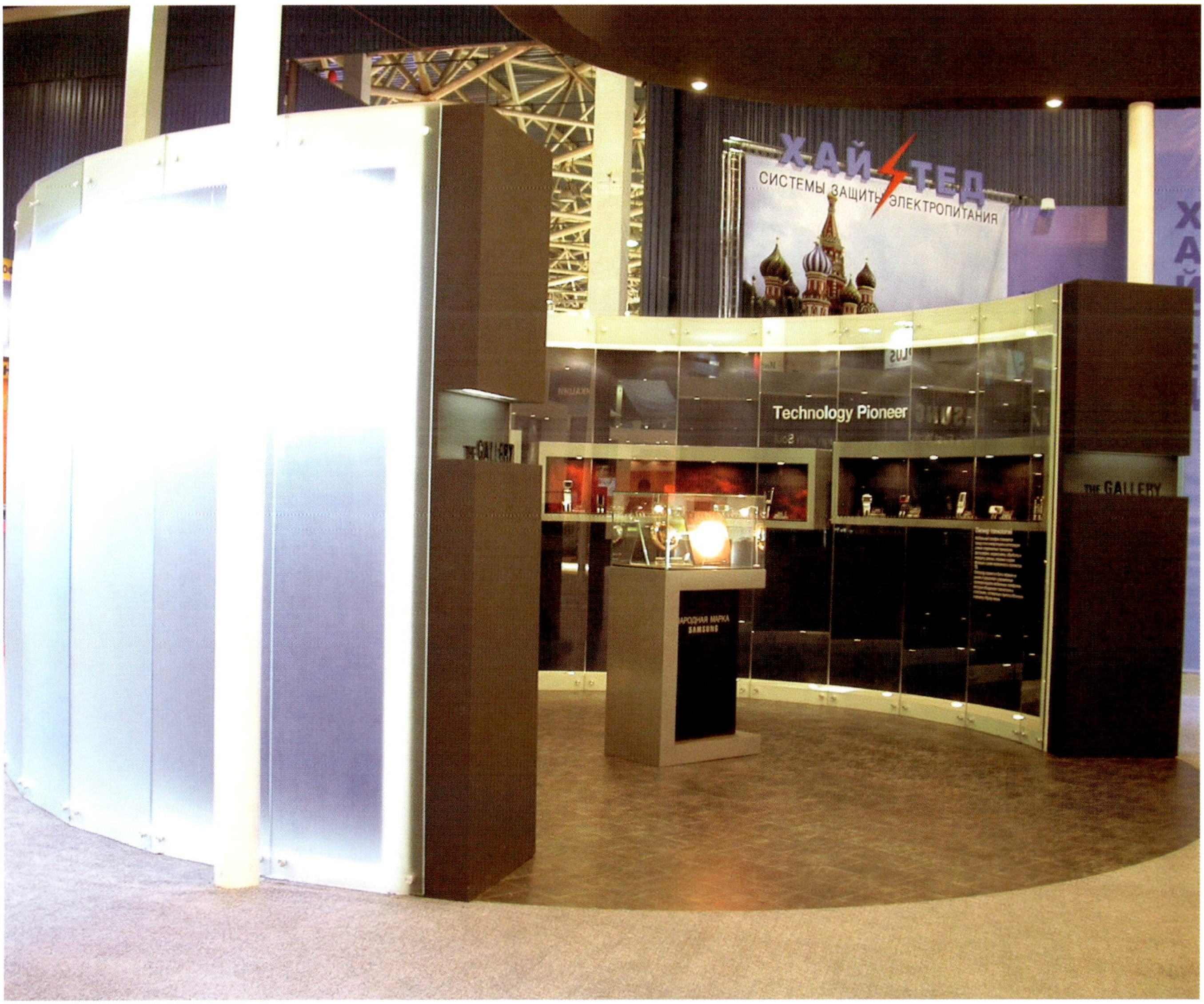

FLEXI

5,300 SQUARE FEET

Sapica, Leon, Mexico
Design & Fabrication: *Freeman Exhibits,*
    Houston, TX
Designer: *Chuck Bunger*
Account Executive: *Tom Short*
Creative Director for Flexi: *Mariano Aguilar*
Photography: *Noe Roa, Leon, Mexico*

According to Mariano Aguilar, Flexi's Merchandising
Director who was also the creative director of this 5,300
sq. ft. exhibit that dominated the 2005 Sapica Show in
Leon, Mexico, "Flexi wanted a space that while being
conducive to demonstrating the latest footwear styles,
would also be a comfortable environment for the Flexi
clients to meet with each other and socialize with the
Flexi management." Chuck Bunger, the designer at

114

Freeman Exhibits—the Houston firm that also constructed the exhibit—was faced with the challenge of creating a warm and productive environment. Also, to safeguard the new Flexi designs from the competition, the exhibit had to be confined behind a perimeter wall—and still be welcoming.

Sapica is the shoe industry of Mexico's major expo/trade show and Flexi is one of the leading manufacturer/retailers of shoes. Tom Short, the account executive at Freeman Exhibits described the booth: "The feeling you have upon entering is like an exclusive oasis in a very congested and noisy environment." The exhibit was contained by a translucent facade and the retailers/clients were greeted at the entrance by a host or hostess, "The entry made a bold visual lead-in with a bright red tensioned fabric canopy that flowed from the far side of the exhibit to the 20 ft. tall entry tower." A serpentine wall, with built-in greenery planters below and frosted Plexi panels above, allowed for an open environment yet maintained the privacy of the individual meeting spaces inside.

Inside, the left hand side of the space was divided into 22 individual stations where salespersons interacted with their clients. The stations were separated by frosted Plexiglas screens and the curved counters/desks surrounded by chairs, were backed up by the illuminated walls where 100 sample shoes were displayed. Custom undulating metal frames with frosted plastic inserts allowed the lighting to extend down to the lower shelves on the wall. "Curves and elliptical shapes were used to soften the boxy perimeter wall." This was evident in the header beams, the shape of the centrally located conference area, the design of the waiting/hospitality area where food and drinks were served to clients waiting to be attended to by the sales staff and in the sweep of the graphic wall that was a focal high point in the exhibit.

Light toned wood laminates, frosted Plexiglas, live flowers and plants and service all added up to "a warm but airy atmosphere." The space had an open, out-of-doors feeling that supported Flexi's comfortable and casual footwear.

flexi
SONY
Discovery
FOX

flexi
flexi

flexi
flexi

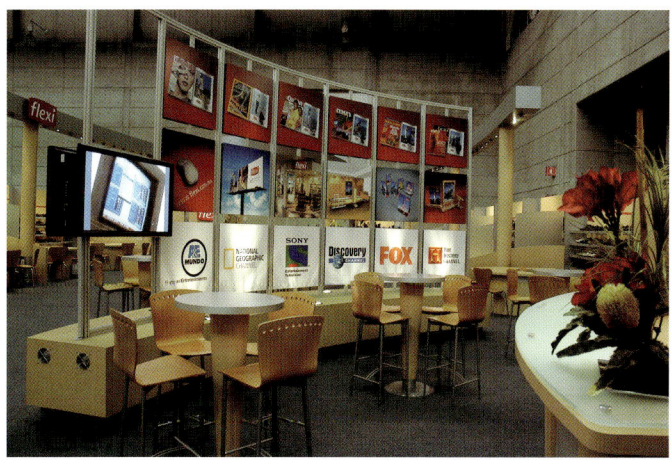

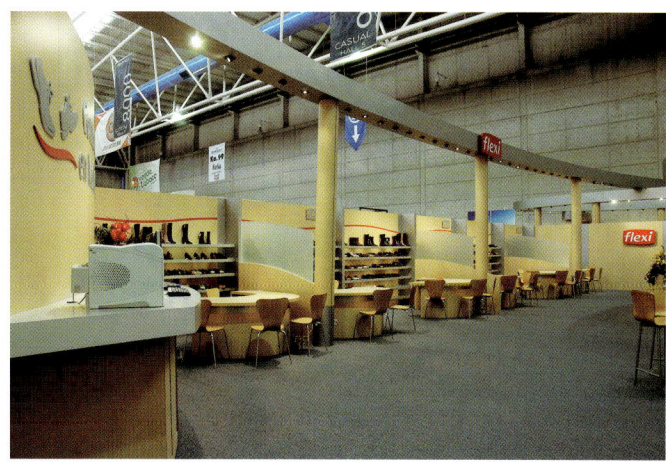

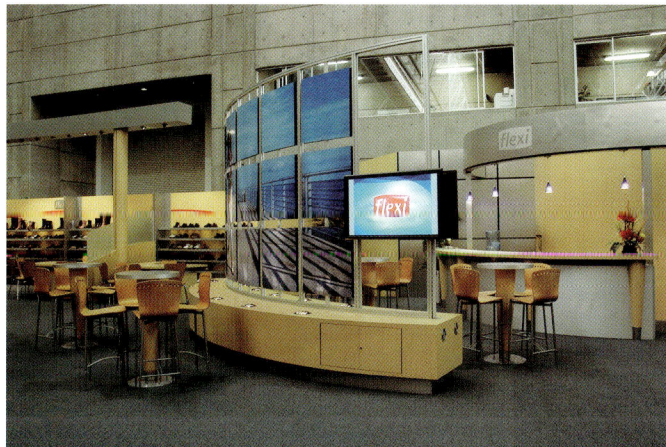

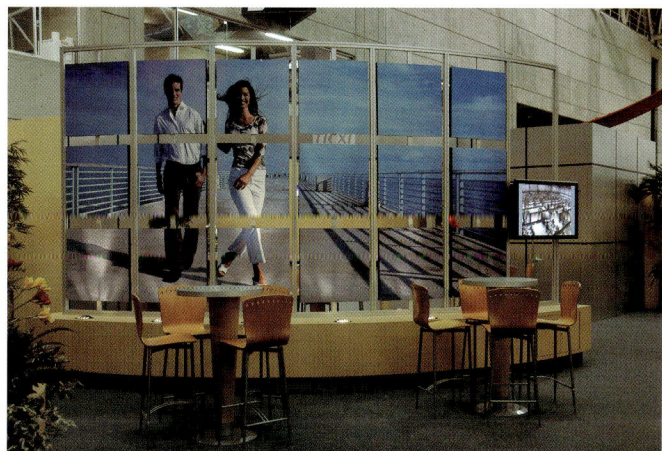

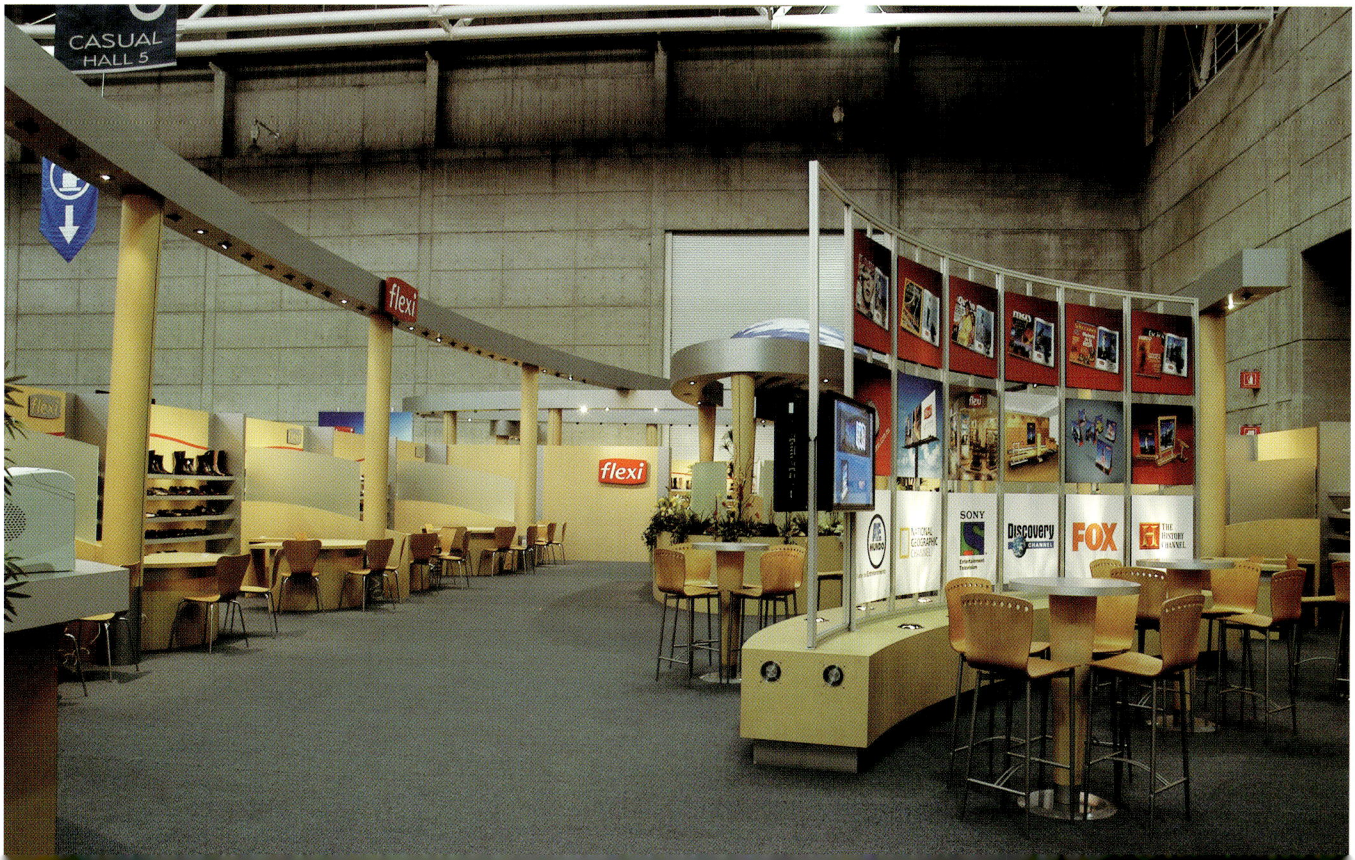
CASUAL
HALL 5
flexi
flexi
SONY
Discovery
FOX

KOHLER

5,700 SQUARE FEET

Kitchen/Bedroom/Bathroom Show 2004, Birmingham, UK
Design: *Checkland Kindleysides, London, UK*
Photography: *Rick Gem*

The 5,700 sq. ft. Kohler stand, designed by Checkland Kindleysides of London, was one of the most prominent and innovative stands at the Kitchen/Bedroom/Bathroom Show in Birmingham, UK.

The basic concept was to divide the stand into three key areas: outer pavilions, inner product stories and a central hub. Theatrical focal points or towers flanked each outer edge of the stand, and these individual pavilions "told a story about a key product range in a unique and engaging way—expressing Kohler's design, innovation, heritage and artistry whilst drawing visitors into the stand." Visitors could "visually and physically" experience Kohler's production techniques in manufacturing cast iron products in the Cast Iron pavilion where graphic imagery was used to dramatic effect. The SOK pavilion highlighted the benefits of chromotherapy through the use of a color changing wall that was sequenced to reflect the radiant palette of the SOK baths. A strong sense of theater was produced through the introduction of an ice sculpture in the Sculpting Water & Form pavilion. The sculpture reflected the design cues of the Escale range. "Through the use of texture, color, form and material, each tower told a different story relating to Kohler's visual range."

Four secondary "stories" were told in the inner core of the stand. Products were grouped around a given theme such as texture or form. Here visitors could, at their own pace, discover Kohler's line and the new product launches in fitted furniture and kitchen sinks.

The hub or core of the stand was designed as a "greeting point between the visitor and the brand—relaxed and welcoming in tone, yet distinctive in design." This area

BRUDERER

EuroBlock 2004, Hanover, Germany
Design & Fabrication: *Syma Systems, Switzerland*
Photography: *Courtesy of Syma Systems*

6,500 SQUARE FEET

Though the space was large—almost 6,500 sq. ft.—Bruderer showcased only one of its machines at Euro-bleck in Hanover, Germany. Syma Systems, who designed and fabricated the exhibit, had not only to feature the new product but had to combine the spacious rest and conferencing areas with dining/hospitality zones, all within a single cohesive design.

The contemporary look was established with the fabric fins or sails that reached out from a central core location to effectively became an open "ceiling" over the space. The sharp, angular thrusts of the sails and the floating ceiling panels were complemented by the semi-circular metal frame and tension fabric partial enclosure in the center of the space that became the focal point of the design. The forward sweep of the information desk, in the company's signature green, repeated the arcs and

BRUDERER

curves that were also apparent throughout the exhibit space and were repeated in the wood slatted screens (Syma Molto) that were used to affect semi-private enclosures on the floor. They also helped to define the perimeter of the stand.

These "enclosures" served as work stations where there were demonstrations in the latest state-of-the-art technology in punching. What was going on behind the screens was partially visible to the attendees on the aisle and the desire to really "see" what was happening brought them

in through the wide openings between the screened areas. The previously mentioned focal semi-circular enclosure served as the major reception/dining/drinking area in the exhibit with a bar as well as widely spaced tables with chairs around them.

Islands of greenery were added to the mainly fabric and metal construction to offer a natural softness. A "tree" grew up in the center of this main enclosure and it was set in a circle of pebbles, rocks and plants in terra cotta planters.

More plants appeared in terra cotta planters throughout the space.

The result: "A great atmosphere with stylish landscaping for a relaxed encounter."

CADENCE

Design Automotive Conference (CAD) 2004,
      San Diego, CA
Design & Fabrication: *MC2*
Photography: *Anna Eglert*

7,200 SQUARE FEET

"This exhibit represented a new, edgier look for Cadence that reinforced its brand image of being the leader who pushes the edge." That's how the designers at MC2, who created the new 7,200 sq. ft. exhibit space that was introduced at the Design Automotive Conference in San Diego, CA, described the look.

Hanging down from the hall ceiling were very large rings that played with different colored lights. The yellow, red and blue color scheme continued to the stretched fabric panels that set the look for the stand's surround. Suspended in front of these colorful shapes were the Cadence logo panels. Together, these shapes, forms and colors created "a modern and sophisticated" ambiance for the interior space. The interior of the booth was furnished with soft, rounded and somewhat retro furniture in "living room" clusters with an occasional table and dining chairs

added. Black circular ceiling grids were dropped down over these groupings to enhance the intimate character of the space. These rings carried "messages" in dimensional letters around their rims. The grids also complemented the hanging light fixtures previously mentioned.

Undulating metal and fabric partitions served as separators on the floor and hanging in front of them were boards for demonstrations. To either side of these "talk-boards" were plasma screens that carried visuals of the company's product range. The seating, previously mentioned, were arranged so that "consultative, peer-led presentations" could be facilitated since—"that is the perfect solution for an industry that prefers advice from a colleague to advice from a salesman." In the seating areas the color palette ranged from off-white and cream to orange and red: warm, rich and friendly colors.

SATURN

9,000 SQUARE FEET

North American International Auto Show, Detroit, MI
Design & Fabrication: *George P. Johnson Co., Auburn Hills, MI*
Design Team: *Chuck Bajnai/Carl England/ Ed Schowalter*
Graphic Designers: *Chris Lusk & Craig Lyons*
Photographer: *Andreas Keller*

80 ft. long illuminated translucent arches spanned the 9,000 sq. ft. Saturn exhibit at the N.A.I.A.S show in Detroit, MI. These dynamic swoops of form and color activated the entire area and created a feeling of movement that filled the space. Under these bridges of light and raised up on platforms outlined with low railings were some of the auto manufacturer's newest designs. Alongside the autos were interactive video kiosks where interested attendees to this show could learn more about the particular auto on display.

In contrast to the warm colors of the lighting that kept changing and moving over the arches and puddling on the floor, the side walls of the space were curtained off with cool blue drapery that made the space seem even larger—and more ethereal than it was. A striking accent was the red "road" that served to strongly demarcate the path of one of the flying arches.

The material palette included resin and aluminum cast flooring as well as areas of woven mesh, resin panels on the soaring aluminum framework of the arches and leather on the vehicle displays and the benches that were provided throughout the space for visitors to rest on before heading on to view another of the Saturn autos on display.

SQUARE ENIX

E3, 2005, Los Angeles, CA
Design: *Volume Design*
Fabrication: *Pinnacle Exhibits*
Photography: *Guy Lewis*

As a leading producer of games, Square Enix needed a "must see" exhibit for their 10,000 sq. ft. space at the E3 show in Los Angeles. Surrounded by colors, pizzazz, flashing lights and all that jazz, Square Enix wanted to stand out—be a destination—and so they called upon Volume Design and Pinnacle Exhibits to create an exhibit that would do just that.

Visitors enter at the front of the space and are led up a long ramp to a large, wide stairway. Reigning above the stairway was a gigantic video screen that was surrounded by sequenced lights. The video wall split in the middle to become a 10 ft. wide entrance way through which —after having climbed the stairway—passed to enter into the theater. "As they did so, they experienced the illusion that

they had walked through a monitor and into a gaming environment."

The wide but shallow 100-seat theater was dominated by the 60 ft. wide projection screen. The fabric canopy overhead "closed in the theater and defined the interior. At such close range to such a large screen, visitors felt that they were inside the games being featured in the multimedia presentation."

As the attendees exited from the theater they were free to experience for themselves the games they had just viewed. There were hands-on demo stations spaced along the long curved wall where guests actually sampled the games.

DAIMLERCHRYSLER JEEP

12,800 SQUARE FEET

North American International Auto Show,
    Detroit, MI
Design & Fabrication: *The George P. Johnson Co.,*
    Auburn Hills, MI
Creative Director: *Paul Hemsworth*
Project Designer: *John Salisz*
Sr. Project Graphic Designer: *Keith Rypkowski*
Photography: *Andreas Keller*

The main thrust behind the 12, 800 sq. ft. exhibit space designed by the George P. Johnson Co. for Daimler-Chrysler's appearance at the N.A.I.A.S. show in Detroit was to launch the new Grand Cherokee Jeep. The use of the Central Park theme was to underscore the concept that Jeep vehicles "possess on-road capabilities in addition to their traditional off-road image."

The single level, aisle stand took on the ambiance of a green space set between rocky outcroppings and a stand of high-rise buildings. The park area between "city" and "mountain" was marked off by a grasslike, textured green carpet. Trees, hand produced of fire retardant materials, were placed throughout the "park" which was accented with fiberglass rocks and a winding road of black rubber that served as the main thoroughfare through the stand. The buildings were constructed of canvas covered wood frames and the forced perspective that was designed into each of these theatrical flats "heightened the sense of depth within the backdrop."

Completing the illusion were the authentic lamp posts, park benches, wrought iron railing, Jeep branded manhole covers on the road and an information desk designed to look like a magazine stand. Much of the design was "theater and imagery." Even the paver stones were hand routed of wood and painted to look like the real thing. These were used along the edge of the road "as a transition to the grass and in the information center to strengthen the most architectural space in the park."

The graphics and signage were designed to work with the cityscape/park theme. Street signs and the magazine covers on the information stand served as the signage. Supported by a 10 ft. by 30 ft. LED wall that depicted the various terrains upon which the Grand Cherokee was at home, an actual Grand Cherokee Jeep showed off its suspension on a driving simulator.

DAIMLERCHRYSLER THAILAND

16,500 SQUARE FEET

Bangkok International Motor Show 2004, Bangkok, Thailand
Exhibit Design: *Multi Designs Co., Ltd.*
Fabricator: *Pico (Thailand) Public Co., Ltd.*
Project Manager: *Vivat Rongkavong*
Project Executives: *Akkapol Panyadilok & Chanida Cholmaitri*
Designer: *Korpong Tramote*
Graphic Designer: *Janat Thiengsurin*
Photography: *Courtesy of Pico Thailand*

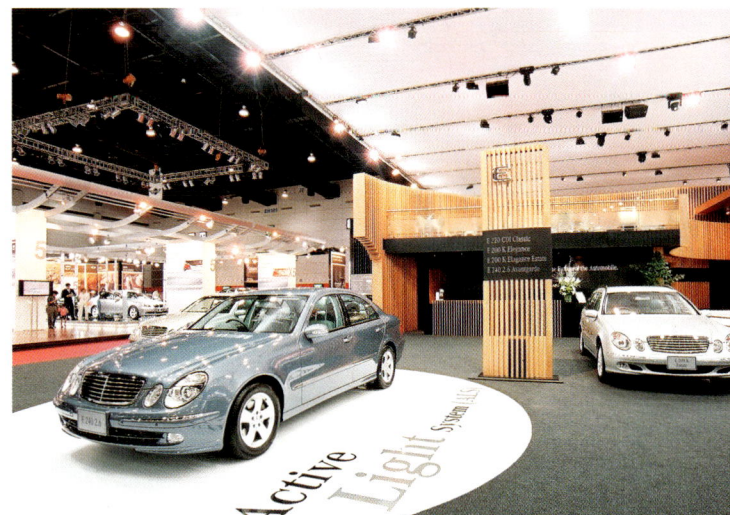

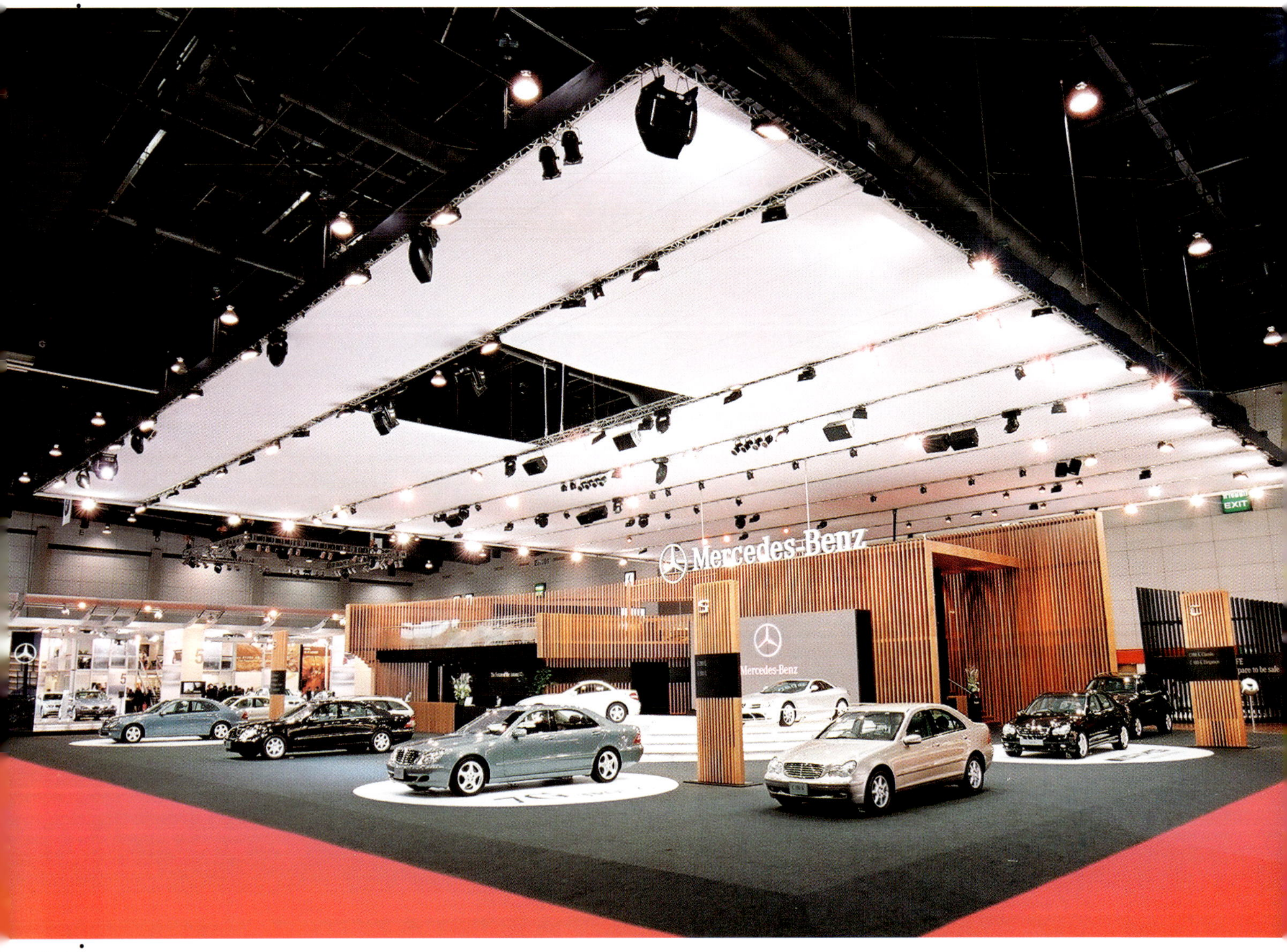

DaimlerChrysler of Thailand made a really big show of their cars at the 2004 Bangkok International Motor Show. The designers at Multi Designs Co. and the fabricators at Pico Thailand had lots of space to work with: 16,500 sq.ft. In the big, spacious exhibit hall this open, clean and wide booth drew attendees from all over the hall.

The designers delineated the space both by the blue carpeting on the floor and the white sails overhead that hovered over the space and camouflaged some of the many halogen lamps that turned the space into a brightly illuminated oasis. Giant white disks were layered over the carpet to "spotlight" some of the featured car models while a series of stepped circles brought attention to other featured models. Two overly-large LED screens slid apart to reveal the new SLK model that was being launched.

The wide open stand was backed up by an all-wood construction at one end: "To create a superior look, warm lighting was used to bring out the golden brown color of the wood. It made the stand rich in color." Housed in this unit was a large dining/entertainment facility as well as areas for conferring with possible clients.

This exhibit was honored with "Best Stand Design & Construction" at that show.

DAIMLERCHRYSLER THAILAND

16,500 SQUARE FEET

Bangkok International Motor Show 2005,
Bangkok, Thailand
Exhibit Design: *Multi Design Co. Ltd.*
Fabrication: *Pico Thailand Public Co., Ltd.*
Project Manager: *Vivat Rongkavong*
Project Executives: *Akkapol Panyadilok & Jaruwan Koedamrong*
Designer: *Korpong Tramote*
Graphic Designer: *Janat Thiengsurin*
Photography: *Courtesy of Pico Thailand Public Co.*

How do you top a winner? The same award-winning team that created the 2004 stand for DaimlerChrysler took on the project for the 2005 show—and in the same 16,500 sq. ft. space.

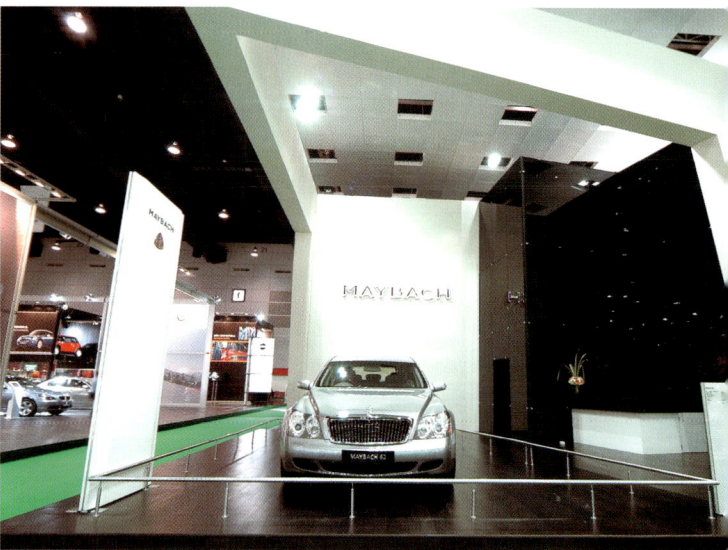

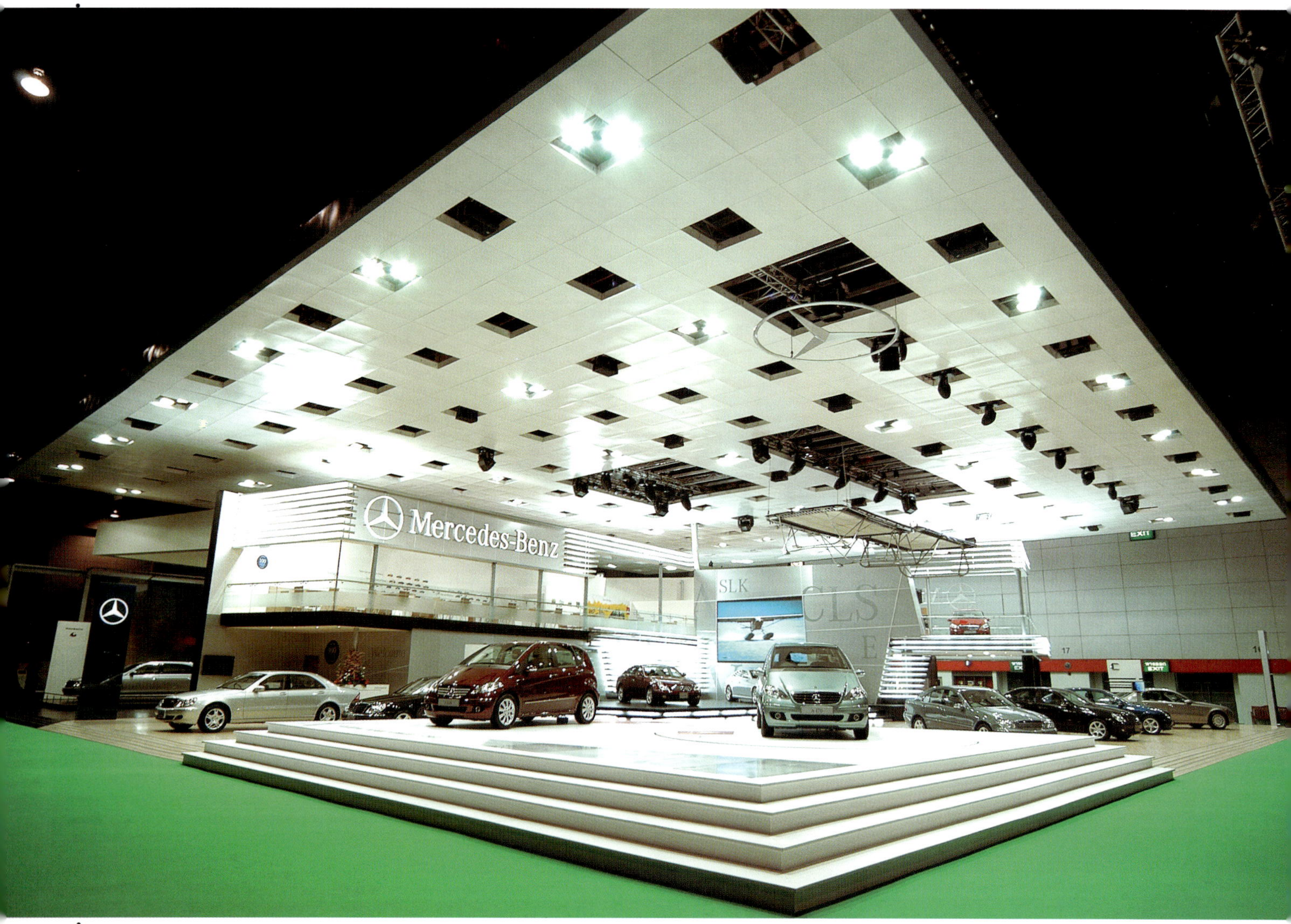

The space was even more evident in the gigantic exhibit hall than previously. Floating overhead was a dropped white ceiling pierced with rectangular openings through which the bright light streamed down onto the multi-tiered platform that covered most of the stand's space. Each step was illuminated from below so that the entire base seemed to glow with light. The central platform was further highlighted with more levels and circular cut-outs in the floor where oversized turntables were recessed. The static autos sitting on the revolving disks were turned into symphonies of graceful motion—and now visible from all angles.

Light colored wood and aluminum were used "to create a superior look" while white was not only used to accentuate the colored automobiles being presented but it was used to affect a "bright, clean, attention-getting look" amidst the clutter and color of the rest of the exhibits in the hall. There were white side walls and the white construction, behind the raised platform, once again served for hospitality and conferencing. Guests sat on the enclosed mezzanine and were able to experience the show put on by dancers and acrobats who performed amid the auto displays, thus turning the autos into "actors" in the ongoing show.

And—once again—DaimlerChrysler's design team walked away with the design award.

CANON

Digital Solution Forum, Las Vegas, NV
Design & Fabrication: *MC2*
Photography: *Jeff Nelle*

For Canon, the Las Vegas Digital Solution Forum is the foremost exposure for the company's products and strategies. It is here that they connect with their dealers. Since it is such an important exposure, Canon asked MC2 to create an impressive exhibit for their 25,000 sq. ft. space at that show where they could show off their wares. The result was a colorful and educational environment that integrated AV and multimedia elements. "The result was that the Canon message was reinforced through an experience that was fun, memorable and very theatrical—all consistent with the Canon brand image."

Giant, soaring fabric and metal framed totems dotted the space—internally illuminated and filled with bright, beckoning colors. The exhibit was planned so that if the attendee stepped through the strongly illuminated and graphically enhanced stand entry and followed the controlled circulation path designed by MC2's design team, the guest would have seen all that there was to see in the booth. For those who were more targeted or product-directed, "the strong messaging hierarchy" created by

the previously mentioned totems helped them to find the product area on the vast floor.

Demonstration areas and interactive stations were set up throughout and here again the signage in the three basic signature colors (cool blue, emerald green and fuchsia) plus white, assisted the visitors in their product search. Seminar "rooms" were created behind look-through screen partitions so that visitors within the Canon stand, but not in the closed-off area, could still partake of what was being shown without being "trapped" within the demonstration space.

138

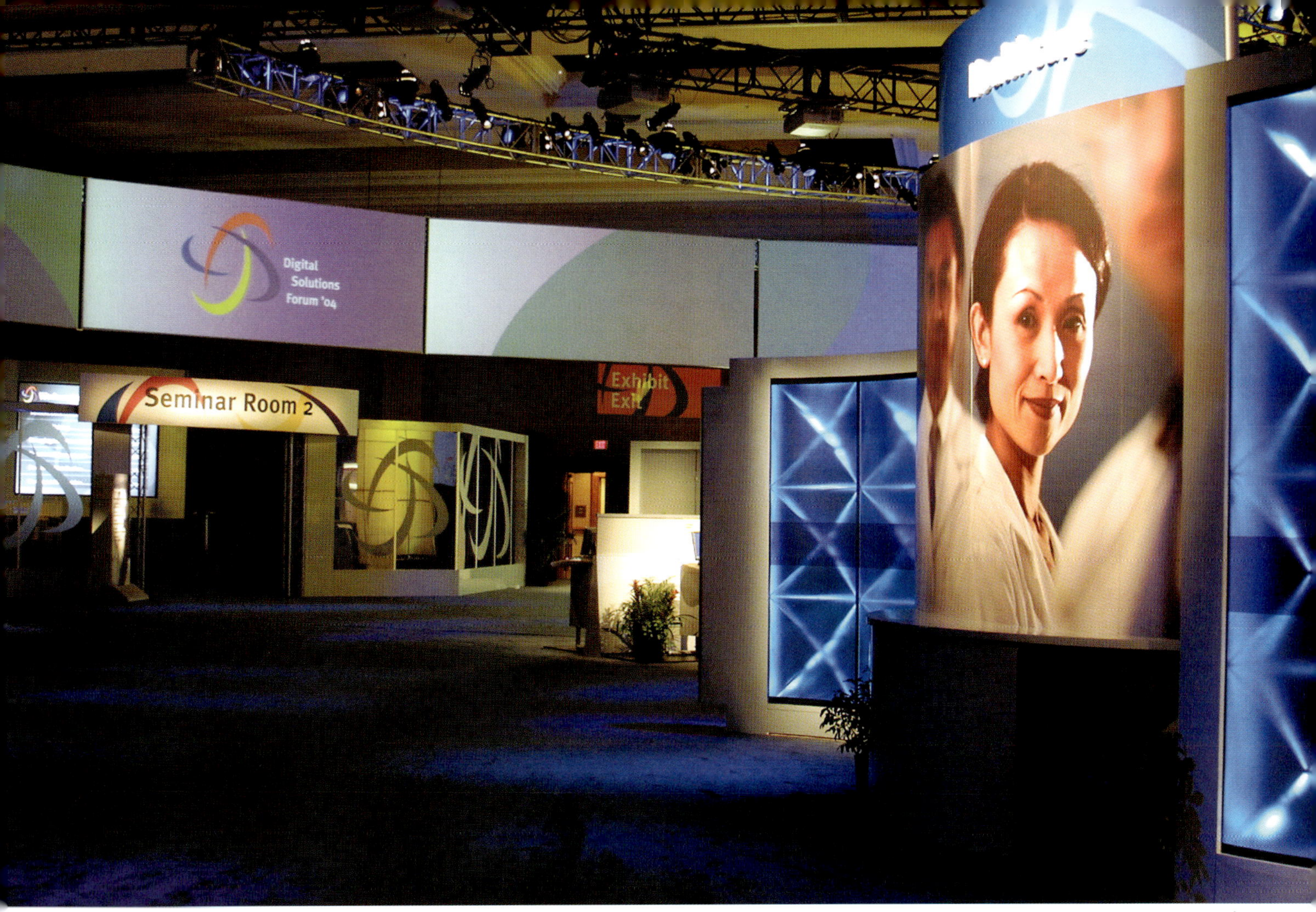
Digital
Solutions
Forum '04
Seminar Room 2
Exhibit
Exit

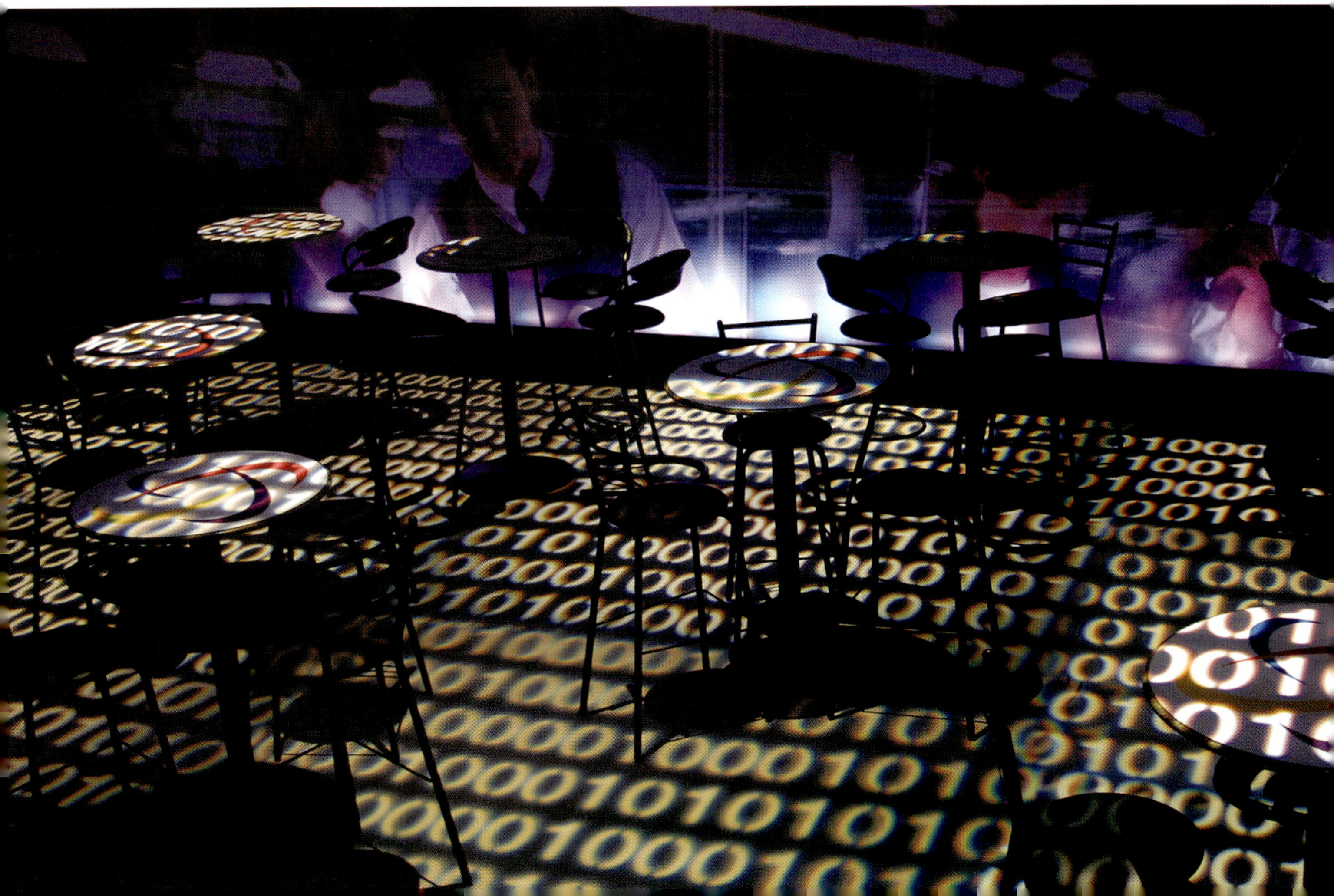

26,000 SQUARE FEET

CES Consumers Electronics Show 2005,
    Las Vegas, NV
Design & Fabrication: *MC2*
Photography: *Jeff Nelle*

Samsung's appearance at the Consumers Electronics Show was a "coming out party." For their 26,000 sq. ft. space they relied upon the designers and fabricators at MC2 to come up with a celebratory design that would say that Samsung was "The Brand" in the consumer electronics field.

The depth, diversity and the quality of the Samsung product line was articulated through the environment's "ethereal, museum-like quality." The wide open plan and the easy traffic flow were combined with the "shrine-like" displays that treated the products as "objects of great value." Circular and serpentine product displays and demo stands seemed to float in the open space that was flushed with changing colors of light. The sprawling exhibit was tied together by the seemingly endless blue

header carrying the Samsung log/name and this illuminated streamer was underscored by a band of video monitors.

Adding to the "festive" feeling as well as the futuristic quality of the design—and the products—there were floating curvilinear canopies with projected images on them that highlighted some of the floor areas while also blocking out some of the hall's ambient lighting. Bright colors and light washers were used throughout to

identify distinct product areas while also contributing to the "party" attitude that Samsung had requested. Adding to the excitement and fun of the stand were the animated screens that appeared providing a sense of movement that complemented the sweeps and arcs of the floor units and the partitions.

PLAYSTATION

E3 2005, Los Angeles, CA
Design: *Mauk Design, San Francisco, CA*
            Mitchell Mauk
Fabrication: *Pinnacle Exhibits*
Photography: *Andy Caulfield*

40,000 SQUARE FEET

The E3 Show in Los Angeles is all about "WOW!!" Every exhibitor does everything possible with color, light and form to "WOW!!" the public—overwhelm them—impress them—shock and awe them. This is all about fun and entertainment and annually Mitchell Mauk and his design team at Mauk Design has the pleasant problem of outdoing his own designs from the year(s) before and once again filling the mammoth 40,000 sq. ft. space with wonderment and awe. Every year the lines get longer and longer with attendees waiting to get into the PlayStation stand to experience its free-for-all visual, play time extravaganza.

For an "opening statement" this year, Mauk created an illuminated helix of side-emitting fiber optics at the first corner of the booth that cycled through a variety of colors and patterns.

"This visual icon primed visitors for the tremendous level of 'wow' waiting for them inside the exhibit." To introduce PlayStation 3, it started with a dramatic walk along a 160 ft. long by 15 ft. high LED screen. It was—at the time of the installation—the largest in the world. The wall was a fabric curtain with LED lights sewn in and thus there were washes of color, pattern and motion. Illuminated railings led the way. In the "waiting room" which was entered through a "pulsing portal,", there was a warm-up video. Once inside the actual theater, guests were "immersed in the capabilities of PlayStation 3 via ultra high resolution video." There was a space-like depth to the theater where patterns on the walls glowed in the ultraviolet light. A shrine-like display of the PlayStation 3 unit rotating within a cylindrical enclosure greeted guests as they left the theater.

There was a pristine rectilinear design to the double deck PlayStation Pavilion where PlayStation Portable was demonstrated. White beamed architecture, an illuminated floor and overhead cloud graphics combined "to create a mystical serenity that contrasted with the high energy atmosphere" of the rest of the exhibit. The neutral palette set off the PlayStation Portable units and enhanced the dramatic colors produced on the ultra bright screens.

There were also rows of spherical transparent hanging chairs. "These unique sound-blocking demo stations enabled each attendee to have an intimate experience with PlayStation Portable"—while other attendees looked on and awaited their turn.

New game titles were featured in molar-shaped enclosures that featured eight demo kiosks. These demo kiosks combines 32 in. LCD screens with minimal structure. Screen shots of the game adorned the inner surfaces of the structures as well as the carpet underneath. "WOW!!"

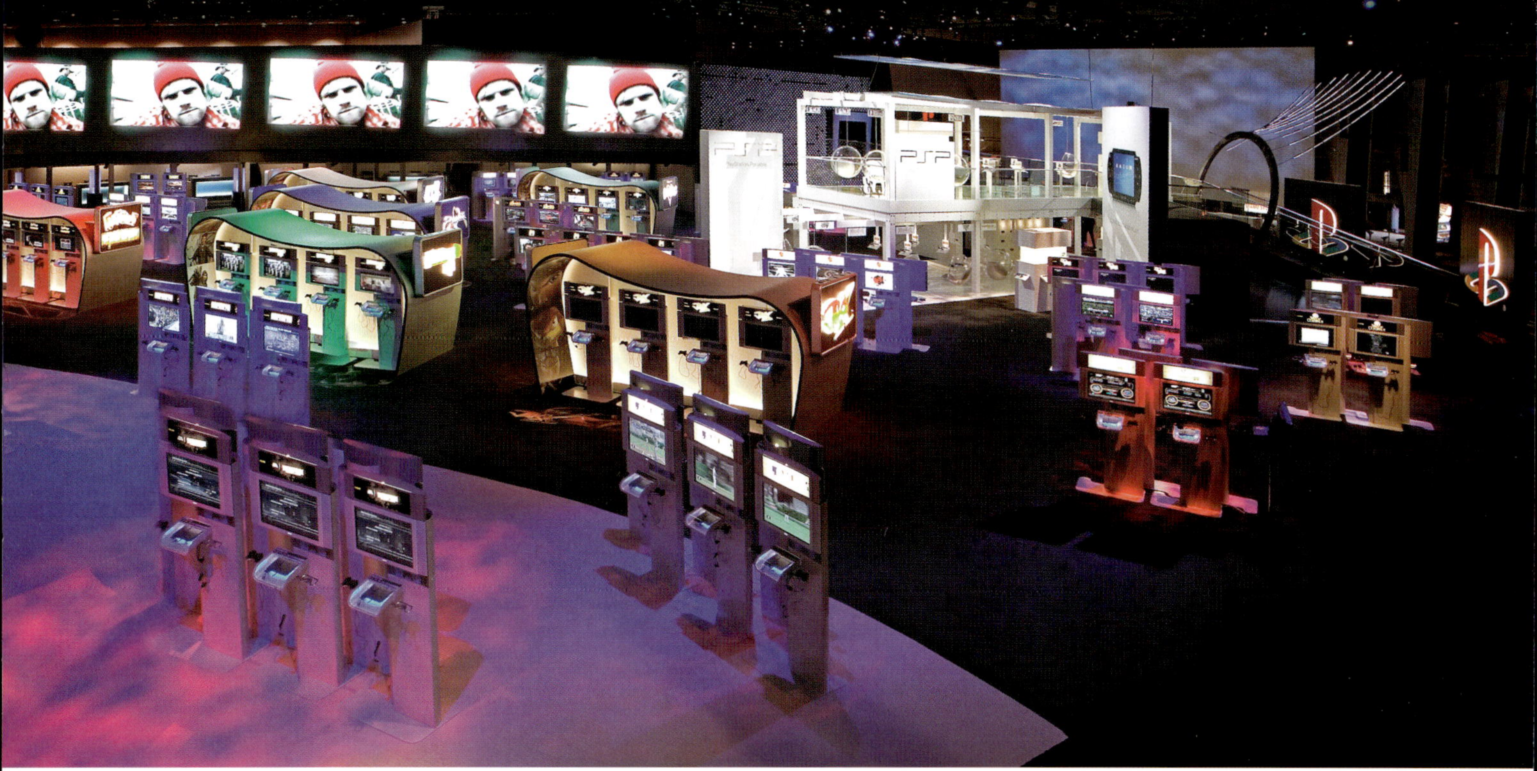
PSP

SOCOM 3
U.S. NAVY SEALS

PSP

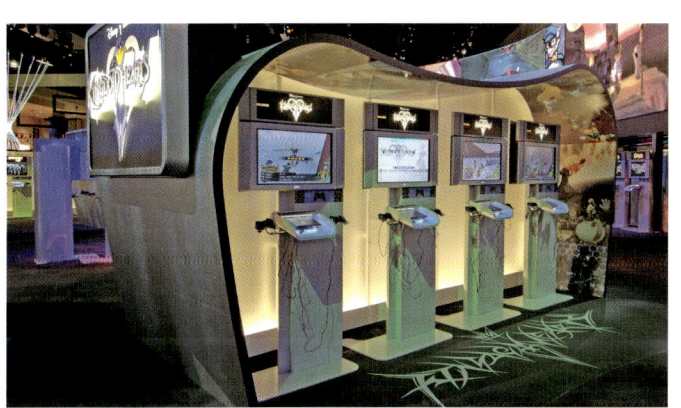

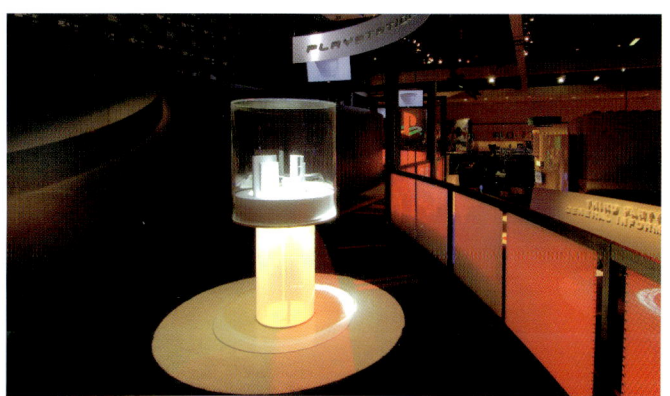

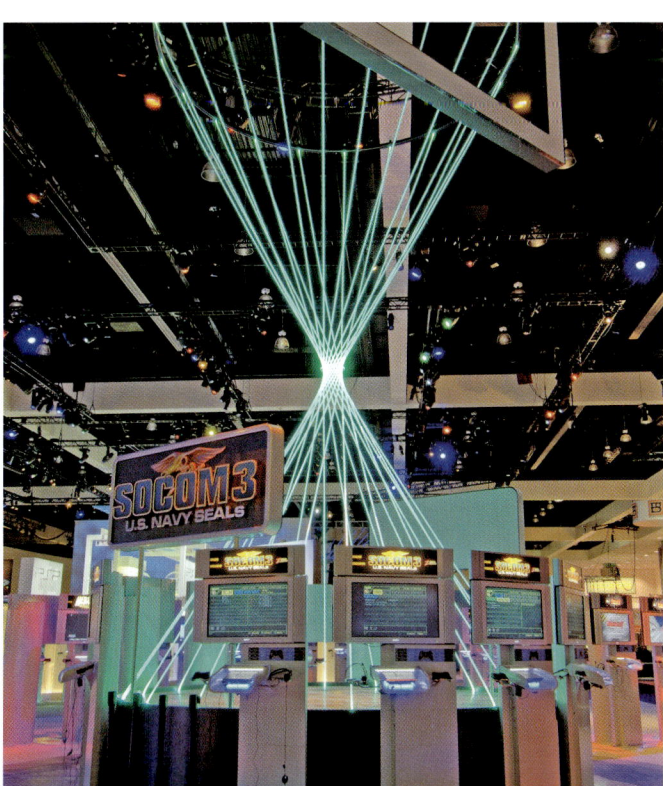

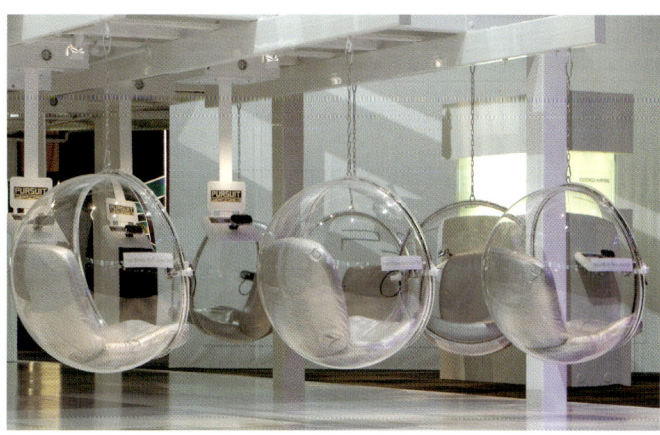

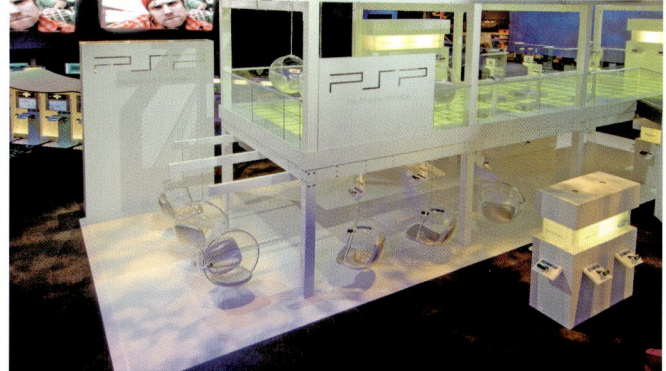

MCWANE NEWSROOM, BIRMINGHAM, AL

2,050 SQUARE FEET

Design: *Lorenc + Yoo, Roswell, GA*
Fabrication: *Designer's Workshop, Atlanta, GA*
Photography: *Rion Rizzo, Creative Sources, Atlanta, GA*

Located in the McWane Center Science Museum in Birmingham, AL, is this 2,050 sq. ft. permanent exhibit created by Lorenc + Yoo, It was designed "to showcase the inner workings of news production and journalism in an engaging and educational manner." The main focus is on print media with a secondary emphasis on multimedia outlets—including broadcast journalism and internet news postings.

Reserved groups are offered several programmed options for this exhibit. Groups may choose to create a newspaper or produce a broadcast of their own. The "newsroom studio" also functions as a multimedia laboratory for workshops in web design and filmmaking. The studio's showcase program is a newspaper created entirely by the Birmingham city high schools and it reports on news in and for the youth community.

The façade, created for the Newsroom Studio, is reminiscent of the art deco building in which the exhibit space is housed. Two deco figures hold an open newspaper between them and fiber optic cables bring changing light colors to highlight them throughout the day. Inside, a large central column contains a space for the program coordinator and editors' desks. The column is surrounded by a series of news monitors that are visible from each workstation. In the reception area, on the left, there is bench seating for "participant strategic meetings." A series of panels on the ceiling allow for a visual enclosure and for soft lighting to be reflected down on the work stations.

Forming a large semicircle around the central column are the 19 work stations—each with internet access. The partitions for these stations resemble "high-tech, art deco with a touch of warmth from the wood panels." Traditional journalism artifacts such as a typewriter, a tape recorder and an old fashioned flash camera are displayed within these spaces—to add to the atmosphere of an old-time newsroom.

STEINHART AQUARIUM

Transition Museum, California Academy of Science, San Francisco, CA
Design: *Thinc Design, New York, NY*
Photography: *Courtesy of Thinc Design*

Thinc Design of New York City was asked to design the transition aquarium since the original one in the Golden Gate Park in San Francisco was closed down and demolished to make way for a new one being built on the same site. This temporary museum is located in a warehouse building in downtown San Francisco.

The 16,000 sq. ft. space—dubbed "The Fish Hotel"—has become "a platform for experimenting with new concepts, exhibits and modes of interacting with the public that will be transferred to the new facility when it is completed." The designers used primarily inexpensive materials, recycled elements from the original aquarium and a flexible exhibit system that allows easy changes in the space. "The aquarium was designed 'inside-out'—blurring the distinction between visitor and husbandry areas and maximizing the potential between aquarium staff and the public."

The new penguin exhibit was constructed out of moveable panels with a 9,000 gallon fiberglass tank. Another highlight is the 20,000 gallon experimental coral reef tank. The 18 ft. deep exhibit is the only structural concrete tank and it is being used as a test bed for coral husbandry, lighting and water circulation and other research necessary for the 230,000-gallon tank that is planned for the new aquarium. The wraparound "touch tank" is also the prototype for one that will be built in the near future. It is now not only entertaining the visitors but serving as a guide to determine the way to show tide pool animals and how they may interact with the public.

All the smaller exhibits were built into flexible rack systems that are easily reconfigured. "These systems, made from inexpensive warehouse shelving, will be used to develop the methods and infrastructure needed for even more flexible, custom-built systems in the new Steinhart."

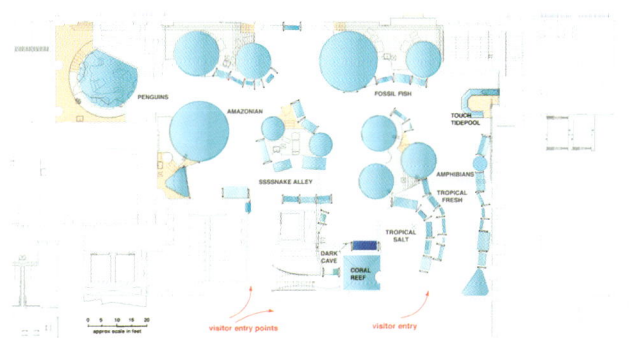

OVERALL PLAN   Transition Facility   July 17, 2003

ANTRON RESOURCE CENTER

NeoCon 2003, Merchandise Mart, Chicago, IL
Design: *Perkins+Will/Eva Maddox Branded*
Environments, Chicago, IL
Design Team: *Eva Maddox/Eileen Jones/Ron*
Stelmarski/Melissa Kleve/Patrick Grzybek
Photography: *Steve Hill, Hedrich Blessing*
Photography, Chicago, IL

The 3,000 sq. ft. Antron Resource Center, in Chicago's
Merchandise Mart, is a year round conference center,
educational facility and office for staff and designers.
Annually it is transformed for the NeoCon trade show
and once again Perkins+Will/Eva Maddox Branded
Environments was called upon to design the new
exhibit that would "build brand awareness and

preference, presentation of its market position and communicate the product family attributes, benefits and features."

The focus of this exhibit was on conveying "The Antron color point of view." With over 360 unique colors in a variety of Antron fiber types and styles, the designers opted for a "sustainable and adaptable modular framework throughout the space." This maximized their ability to reconfigure rooms, display messages and walls while still maintaining power, data and the A/V infrastructure. Fiber samples were shown in hands-on display components: visitors were invited to touch and engage in the color selections. To further enhance the color story, carpet samples from over 20 mills that use Antron fibers were featured as displays and as floor covering applications.

Cardboard tubes of assorted diameters, painted white, were clustered into interesting patterns against white wall partitions. The assorted colored yarns were nestled within these dimensional frames. Other samples were presented as knops—twisted bundles of yarn—inserted through openings in a translucent plastic panel that was supported from below. The "traffic patterns" were set with colored strips of inlay in soft green and warm blue and long hanks of twisted yarn, in a variety of colors, affected a most unusual "forest" through which guests wended their way.

On the wall behind the floor samples that were viewed through cutout panels, the dotted pattern of the cut tubes was graphically interpreted in gray on gray and accented with the blues and greens that were the main colors of the overall exhibit along with white and gray.

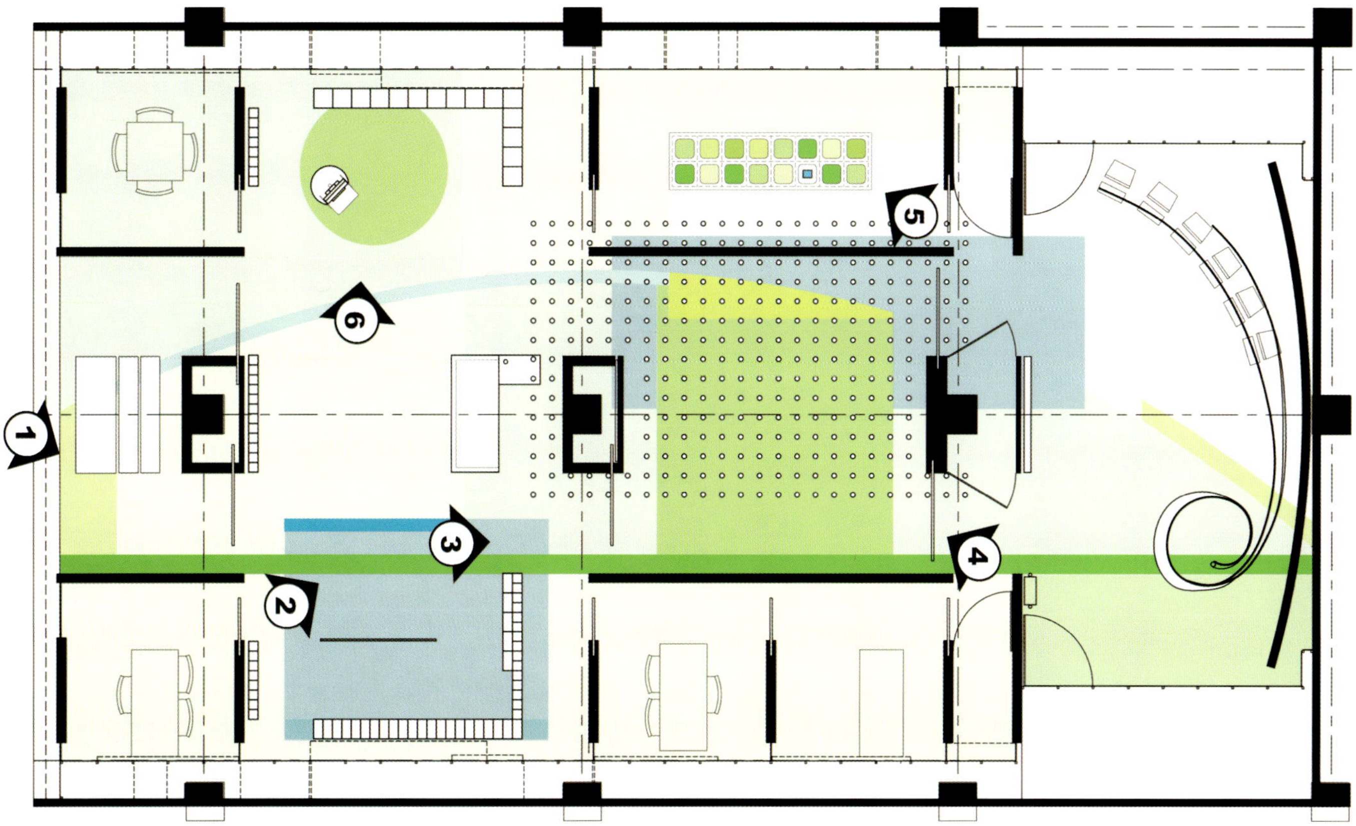
1
2
3
4
5
6

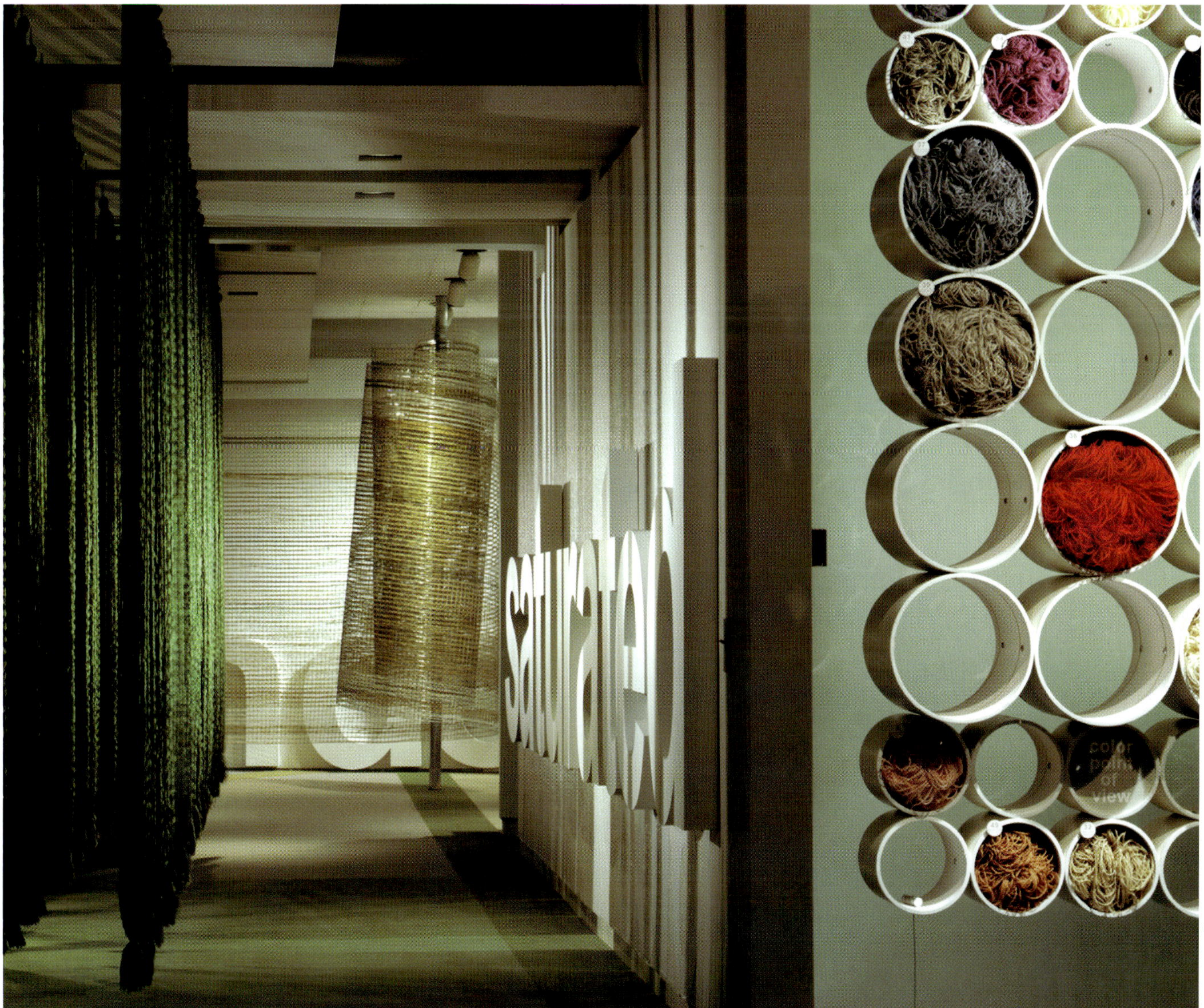
saturated
color point of view

ANTRON

3,000 SQUARE FEET

NeoCon 2004, Merchandise Mart, Chicago, IL
Design: *Perkins+Will/Eva Maddox Branded*
Environments, Chicago, IL
Design Team: *Eva Maddox/Eileen Jones/*
Anna Kania/Melissa Kleve/Brian
Weatherford/Patrick Grzybek
Photography: *Steve Hill, Hedrich Blessing,*
Chicago, IL

For the 2004 NeoCon show Perkins+Will/Eva Maddox Branded Environments once again accepted the challenge of creating an all-new, all-different, yet Antron-promoting exhibit in the 3,000 sq. ft. of the Antron Resource Center in the Chicago Merchandise Mart.

The theme for this showing of Antron fibers and colors was "Makes all the difference in the world." Integrating strategic brand planning, marketing communications, interior architecture, exhibit display and environmental graphics, the design team "utilized an holistic approach to maximizing Antron brand impact within the environment—building an emotional tie with the customer."

As the visitor entered, he or she was faced with four "questions." The "answers" to these questions were revealed as the visitor wandered through the space and—in a most engaging manner—was introduced to the fundamental qualities of Antron. Secondary displays and communication elements were used to build a preference for the Antron brand through the presentation of the company's market position and illustrations of the product's attributes, features and benefits.

The space was organized in "a linear pathway" and made use of a tunnel-like element as a special organizer. The fiber displays led the visitor from the corridor through the space and then back out. A three dimensional modular framework system was used throughout while bold, unconventional and unique "fiber objects" or "sculptures" were used to express the four aspects of Antron: these were the "answers" to the "questions" posed up front. "Blurred imagery and graphic treatment were built upon the visual aspect of the new collateral elements."

BMW DYNAMICS 3 ....

The Padang, Singapore
Design & Fabrication: *Kingsmen, Singapore*
Photography: *Marcus De Photography*

A three story high pavilion with a total of 5,600 sq. ft. of space was erected in the Padang, in Singapore, by Kingsmen Exhibits to launch a new BMW auto. "The client wanted a unique and classy launch that would reflect the new car's high-tech, futuristic and design-oriented feel." The pavilion was conceptualized and constructed in less than a month and two of the new BMW's 3 series automobiles appeared on the second level of the construction.

The pavilion is a "perfect cube" constructed of a modular system and it combined large glazed areas with solid and translucent tones. 1,800 fluorescent lamps turned the pavilion into a glowing white unit, "Using white as a dominant color gave the pavilion a clean yet sophisticated look that is common to all BMW exhibits and showrooms." Barrisol, a very strong and glossy material, was imported from France and used for the ceilings. Lightweight and reusable, it added to the overall look of the interior structure.

Also imported from France for the launch that lasted only two weeks was a DJ. To serve up a truly "multi-sensory experience," there were plasma monitors throughout the space, soft lounge seating, rotating lights and light refreshments and drinks amusingly served up in Petri dishes and test tubes.

Dynamics 3

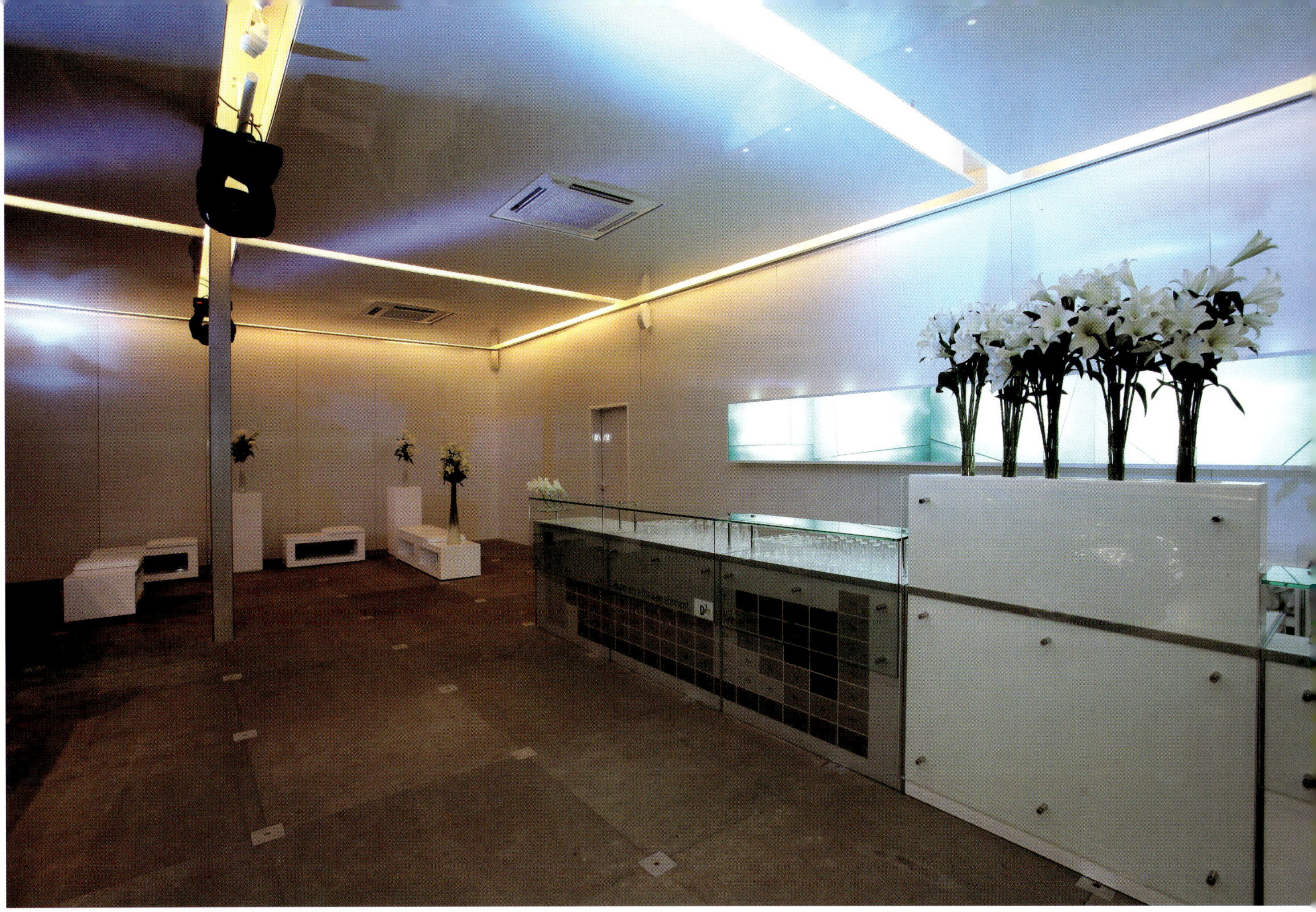

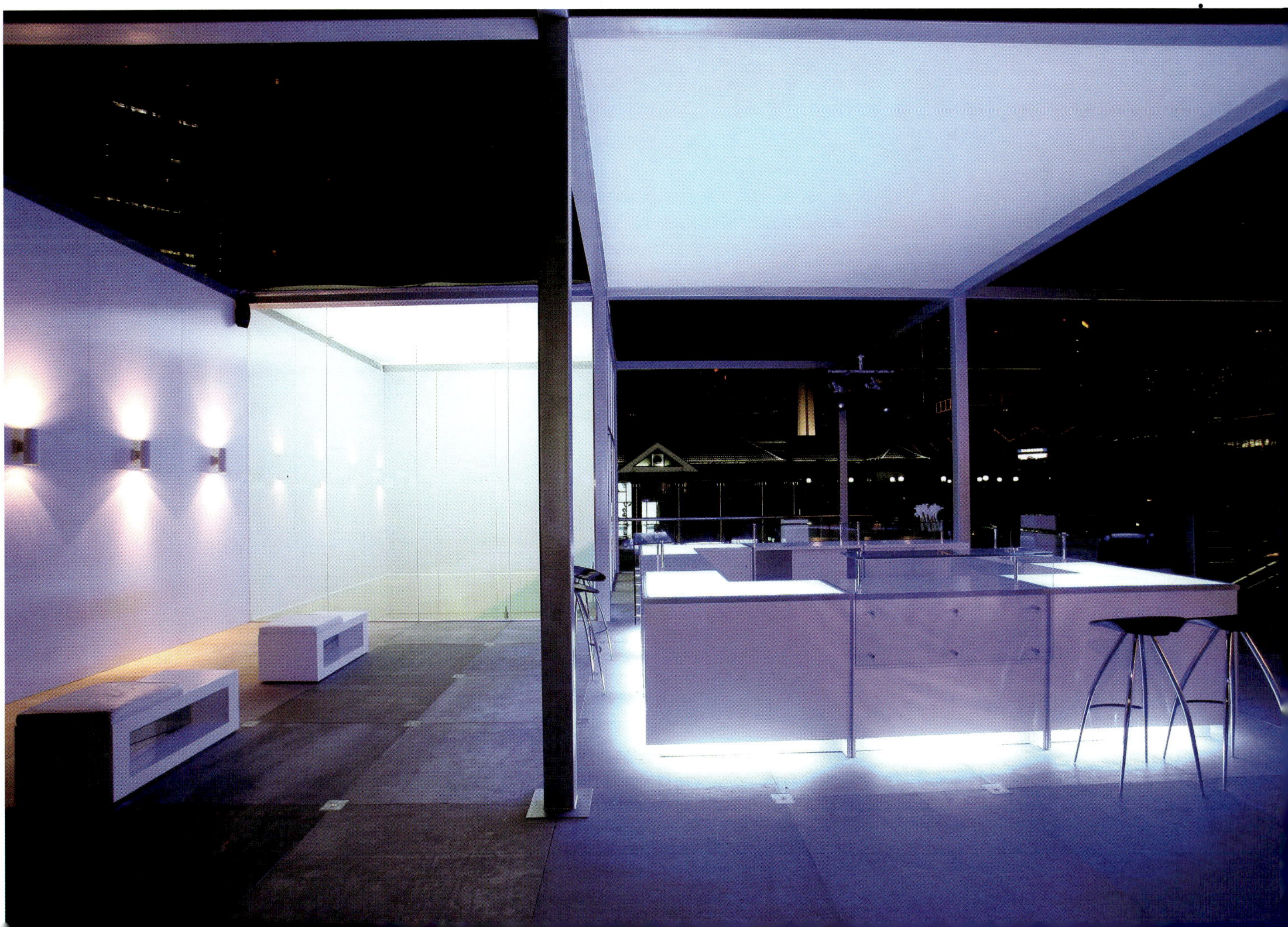

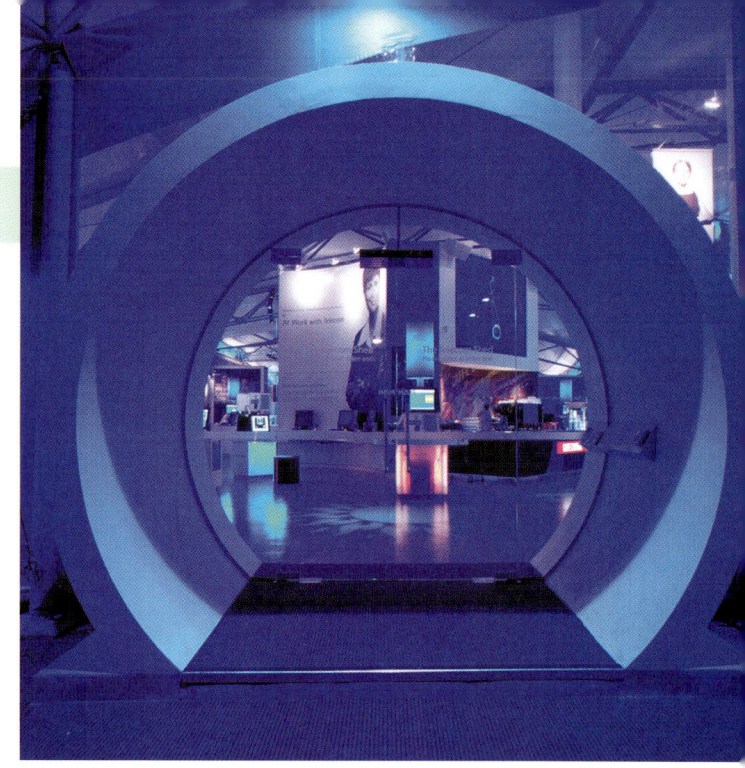

TELECOM NZ

7,400 SQUARE FEET

The Shed Exhibition Environment,
Aukland, New Zealand
Design: ***Landini Associates, Aukland, New Zealand***
Design Team: ***Mark Landini/Paul Gates/ Clayton Andrews***
Photography: ***Courtesy of Landini Associates***

The Telecom "shed" was conceived as a temporary structure by Landini Associates and it was originally planned to be up for six months in the heart of the Aukland Harbour. Since Telecom NZ is a major sponsor and supplier to the "America's Cup" races—the highlight of the world yacht-racing calendar—it seemed that the Harbour was a logical place to be seen and for the company to be represented.

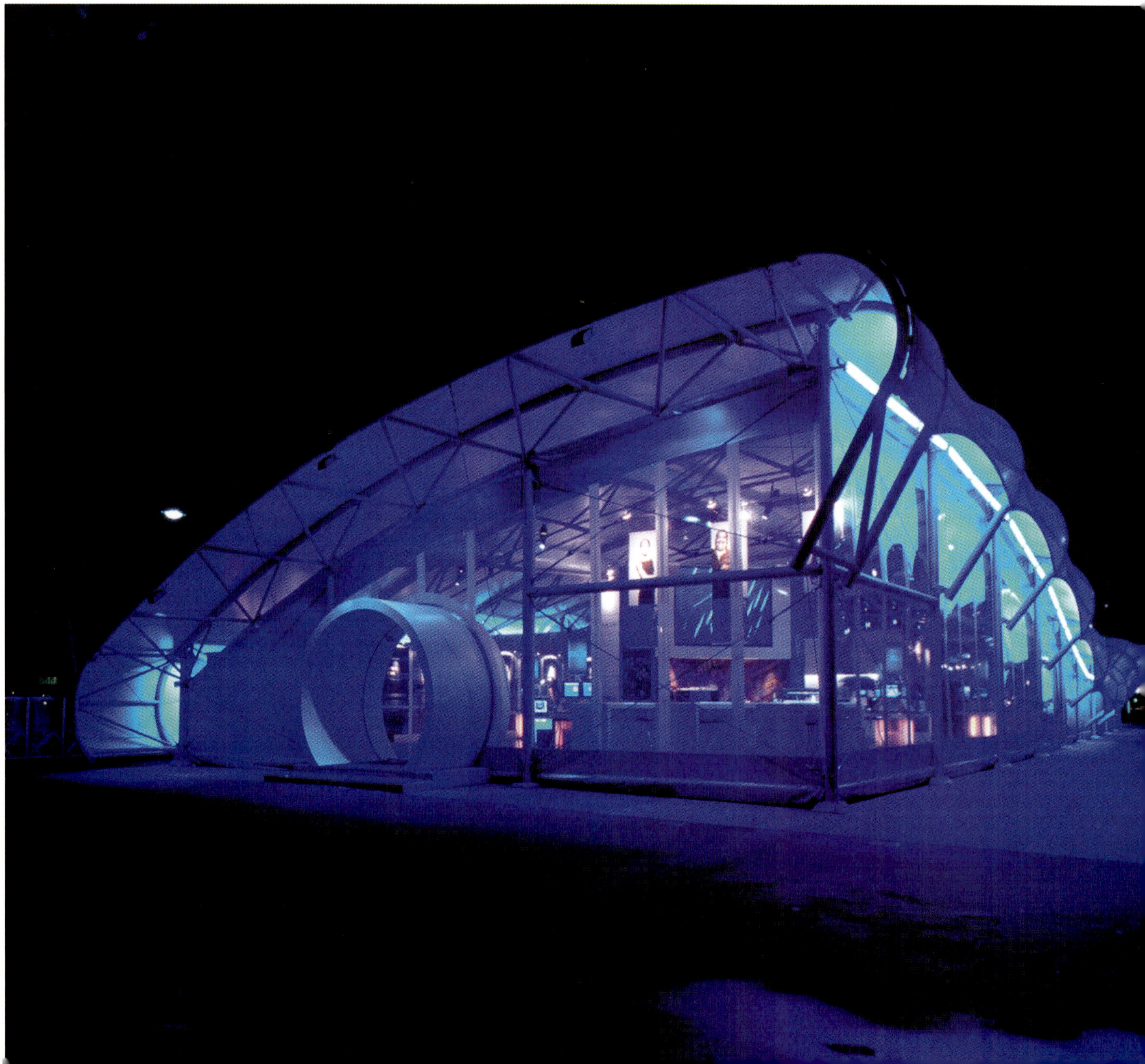

The 7,400 sq. ft. shed is an interactive fusion of sailing and communications: past, present and future. It was designed as more than just a place to be a spectator but where visitors could "meet the team, experience the technology, and understand and experience the race." The design solution helped to shift the audience perceptions of TNZ (Telecom New Zealand) through strong association with innovative technology and cutting edge design.

The skeletal shed with wave-like contours and wide expanses of glass is filled with an eerie blue light—making it almost an underwater experience. Guests pass through a tunnel-like entrance—similar to a decompression chamber—into an exhibit hall filled with interactive kiosks and translucent, glowing in the blue light work stations. Oversized graphic panels reinforce the

"story" that is being presented on the angled stands along the perimeter walls. Spotlights, attached to the overhead arched truss structures, point up the wall graphics as well as the giant suspended graphics printed on fabric that serve to define the various areas on the floor.

In its first six months this exhibit was the biggest attraction in the Harbour and it drew over one million visitors. It has remained open and has also remained a top-draw attraction in New Zealand.

Tactically, the start involves
aggressive use of rules and
practised offensive and
defensive strategies.
Crews will employ a philosophy
similar to a fighter pilot trying
to win a dogfight against an
enemy aircraft.

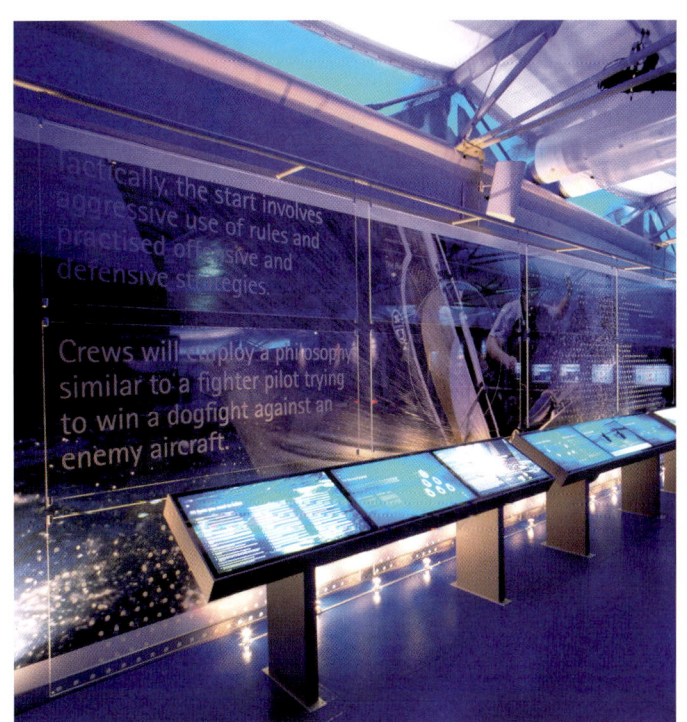

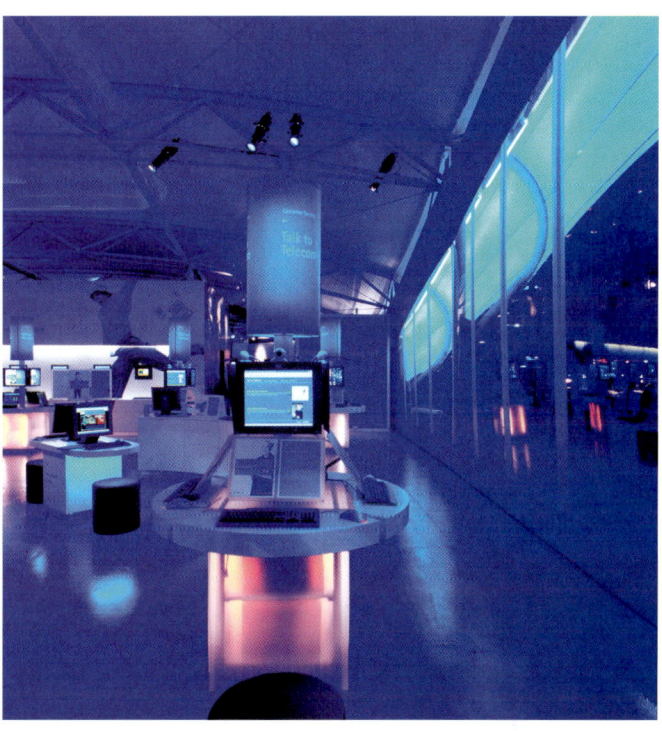

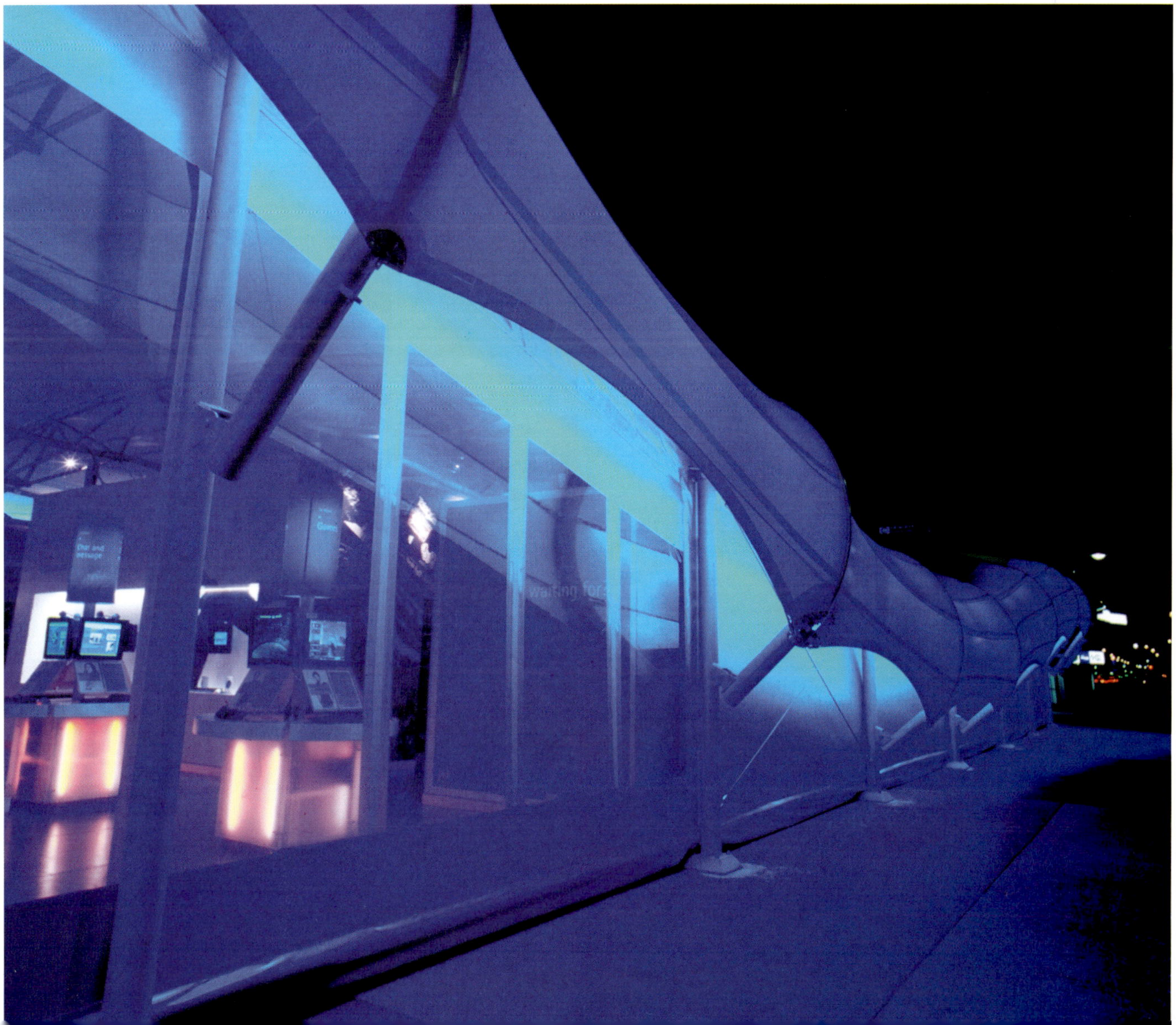

MOTOCROSS AMERICA

8,000 SQUARE FEET

Motorcycle Hall of Fame, Pickerington, OH
Exhibit Design Environment: *Studio Mantra & DeShetler Design*
Design Director: *Maribeth Gatchalian, Studio Mantra*
Exhibit Graphic Designer: *De Shetler Design*
Design Director: *Dean De Shetler*
Fabrication: *Curtis Elliot Designs*
For the Museum:
Executive Director: *Masrk Mederski*
Curator: *Ed Youngblood*
Photography: *Michael Houghton*

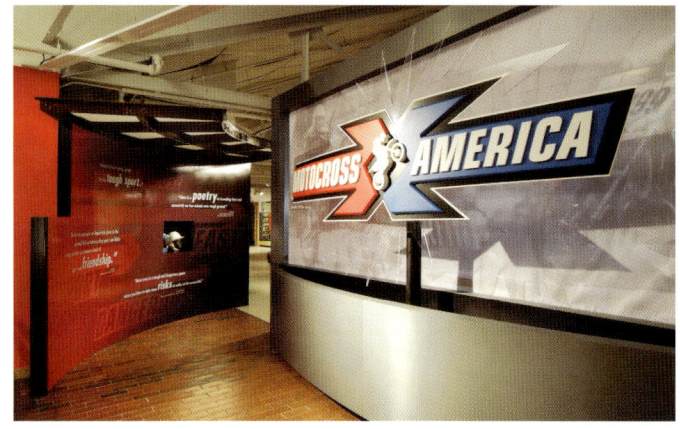

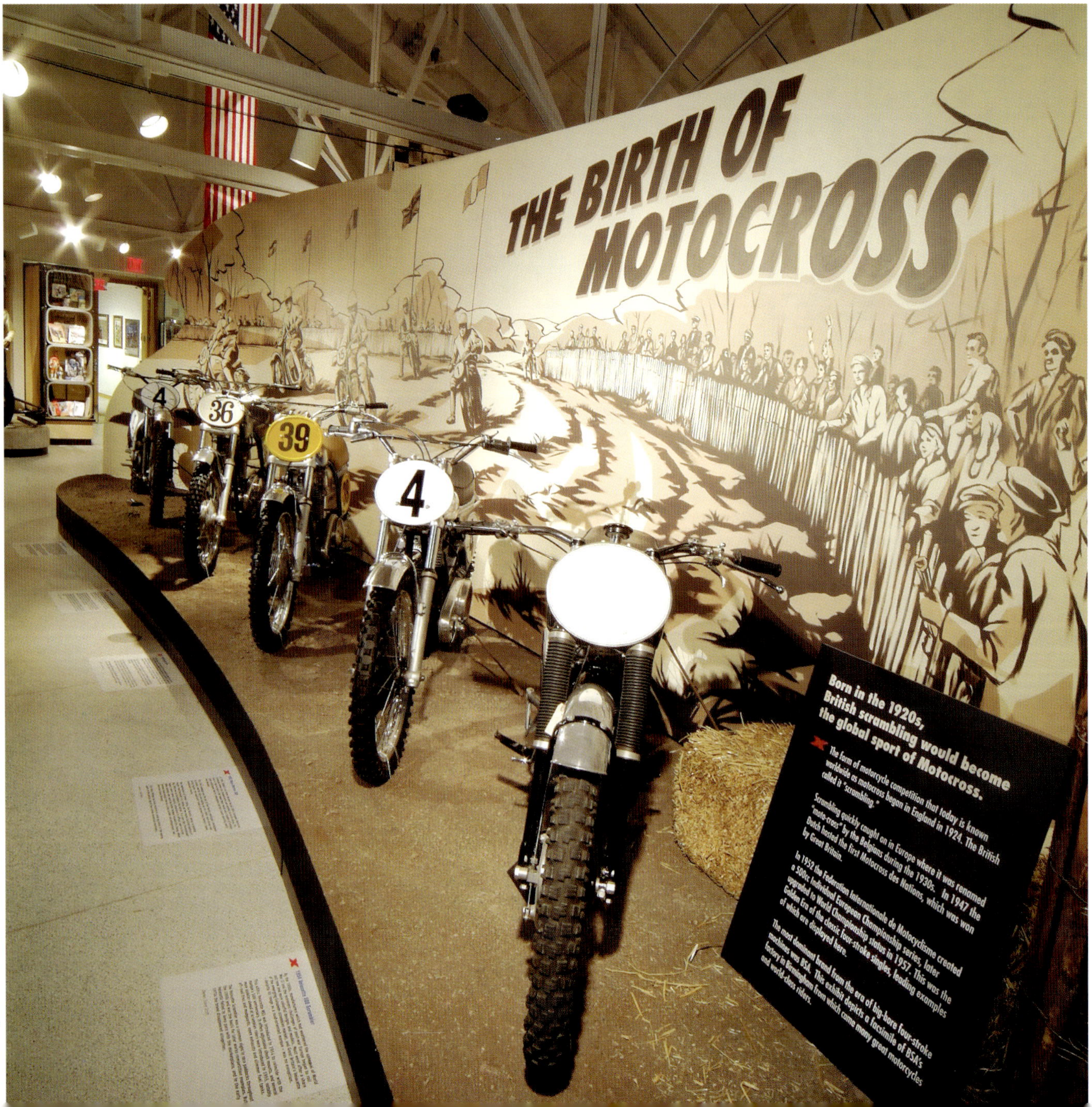

Using over 500 artifacts,, 60 motorcycles, two projection videos with audio, three interactive kiosk stations, seven dioramas and 120 photographs, Dean DeShetler and Maribeth Gatchalian created an exhibit that traced the evolution of Motocross from its 1920's roots in Europe to "today's wildly popular Supercross and free style events in the U.S." Set out over two floors and 8,000 sq. ft. in the Motorcycle Hall of Fame Museum in Pickerington, OH, it shows off "the sport's colorful characters and stories, the cuttng edge technology and gear, and the high energy lifestyle surrounding it."

The concept evolved from a script outline prepared by the Museum's curator, Ed Youngblood. In the design process Dean DeShetler was joined by Maribeth Gatchalian of Studio Mantra and the result, shown here, takes the visitor back in time to 1920 and through visual details, photographic images, historic artifacts and the distinctive sounds of the Motocross bikes, brings the visitors up to the present moment in time. The graphics and 3D environments are integrated . It starts in the "Historic Zone" where the earthy color palette is combined with raw, exposed materials to simulate the early grassroots of a dirt Motocross track. The visitor views the passing years and ends up at the "Modern Zone" where Jeremy McGrath's bike bursts through the 12 ft. high "X" wall at Supercross "signifying the dramatic turn in the sport moving its focus from competitive racing to "X-treme Entertainment."

MOTORCYCLE HALL OF FAME
91

THE EXPLOSION OF
SUPERCROSS
With the advent of Supercross, America applied its unique sports entertainment mentality to the sport.
FOUNDERS HALL

Here the area swells with bright colors and lots of metallic shine. Interactive displays and projected wide screen video walls further entertain and educate the visitor.

Among the unique features in this exhibit are the 30 ft. mural that depicts the first "Motocross des Nations" race, a behind-the-scenes trailer hitch, and side lines of the crew pit, and a simulated dirt track. There is also the motorcycle engine soundtrack that draws viewers into the actual race shown on a large screen, and the "woop di woop" jump of bicycles flying over the open stairwell that connects the two levels of the exhibit.

Mark Mederski, Executive Director of the Museum said, "Don't make the exhibit look transportable and temporary even though it has to be." So, though the exhibit will be dismantled and reassembled in four other locations and then sent overseas, there is nothing the least bit "temporary" about the installation.

GEORGIA PACIFIC

Georgia Pacific Distribution Center, Atlanta, GA
Design: *Lorenc + Yoo, Roswell, GA*
Fabrication: *Designer's Workshop, Atlanta,*
    GA & MDM Scenery Works
Collage Contractor: *Ken McGraw, Atlanta, GA*
Photography: *Rion Rizzo, Creative Sources,*
    Atlanta, GA

As a major feature in Georgia Pacific's re-engineering strategy, a 10,000 sq. ft. exhibit was set up in the company's Atlanta Division Sales Center. As designed by the designers at Lorenc + Yoo of Roswell, GA, the focus was to satisfy the client's "communication objective" and to "explain the sales and distribution process, show as many products as possible, and demonstrate the connection between products and people—the customers."

One of the physical problems the designers had to overcome was not so much the limitation of space as the low, nine foot ceilings. Also, the space overlooked the beautiful Chattahoochee National Forest. "Tight space to build in; vast space to overlook."

The solution involved the creation of six "billboards" upon which the G-P story was unfolded. Using the product as the focal point, the collages used samples of every product the company produced. The Lorenc + Yoo design team employed "visual, tactile and even audible stimuli as a link between products, process and customers." Historic photographs, unfinished logs, window

GEORGIA PACIFIC

frames, wood saw blades, phones and telephone wiring, giant wheels, truck tires, cartons, toy trains and trucks, the exhaust pipe and muffler of a diesel truck, all became the bits and pieces that went into the collages created on the billboards.

Each billboard told a another part of the G-P story starting with the "Company Vision" up front , leading to "Sales," "Logistics," History & Present," and a "Product Collage." The three dimensional collages were full of color, texture and the recognizable objects that had an almost "toy-like quality." However, the well done, but not overdone, graphics provided sound information. Also, visitors could still enjoy the beauty beyond the exhibit since the designers used transparency and lighting effects to enable visitors to see beyond the billboards.

The designers described the exhibit as "a highly kinetic exhibit where the design maximizes the small space without overpowering it, and communicates rather complex issues in an engaging and memorable way."

1965
1956
1953
1949
1970
1960
1950
1974
1963
1955
1951
1948

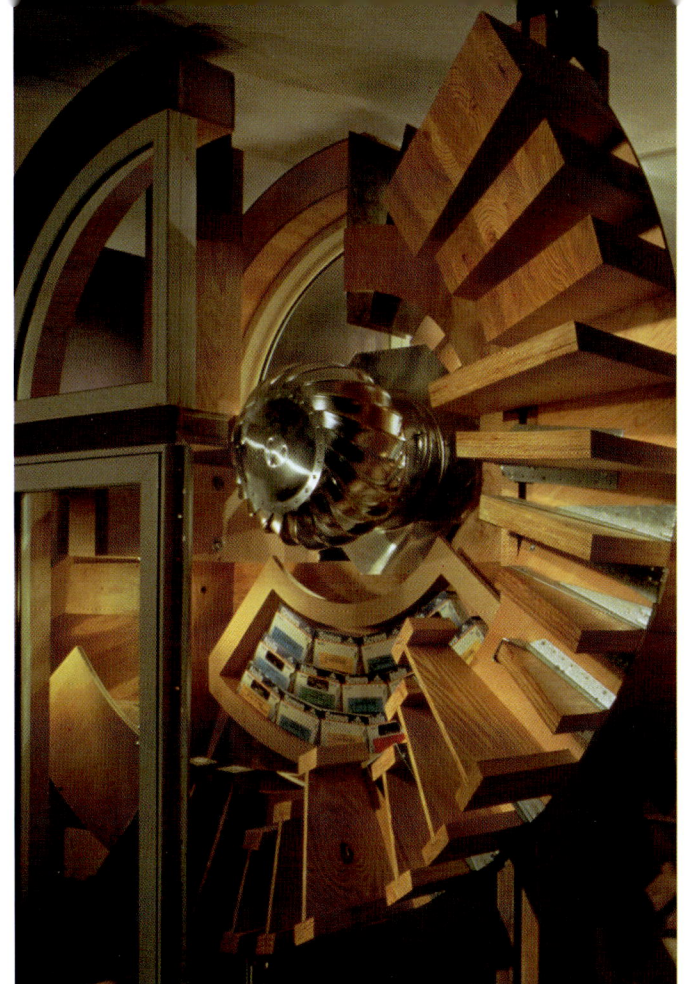

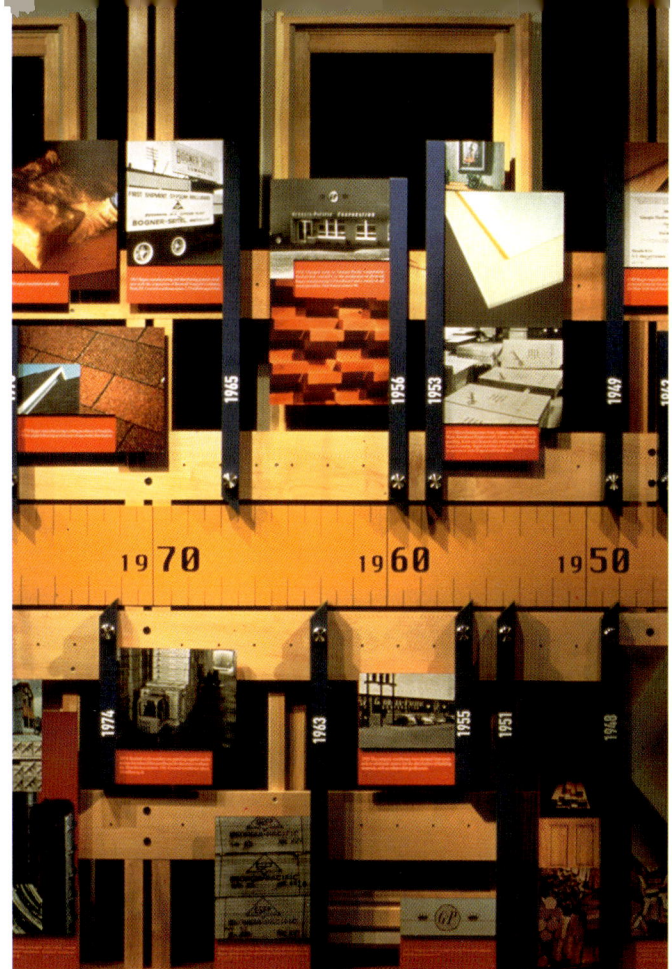

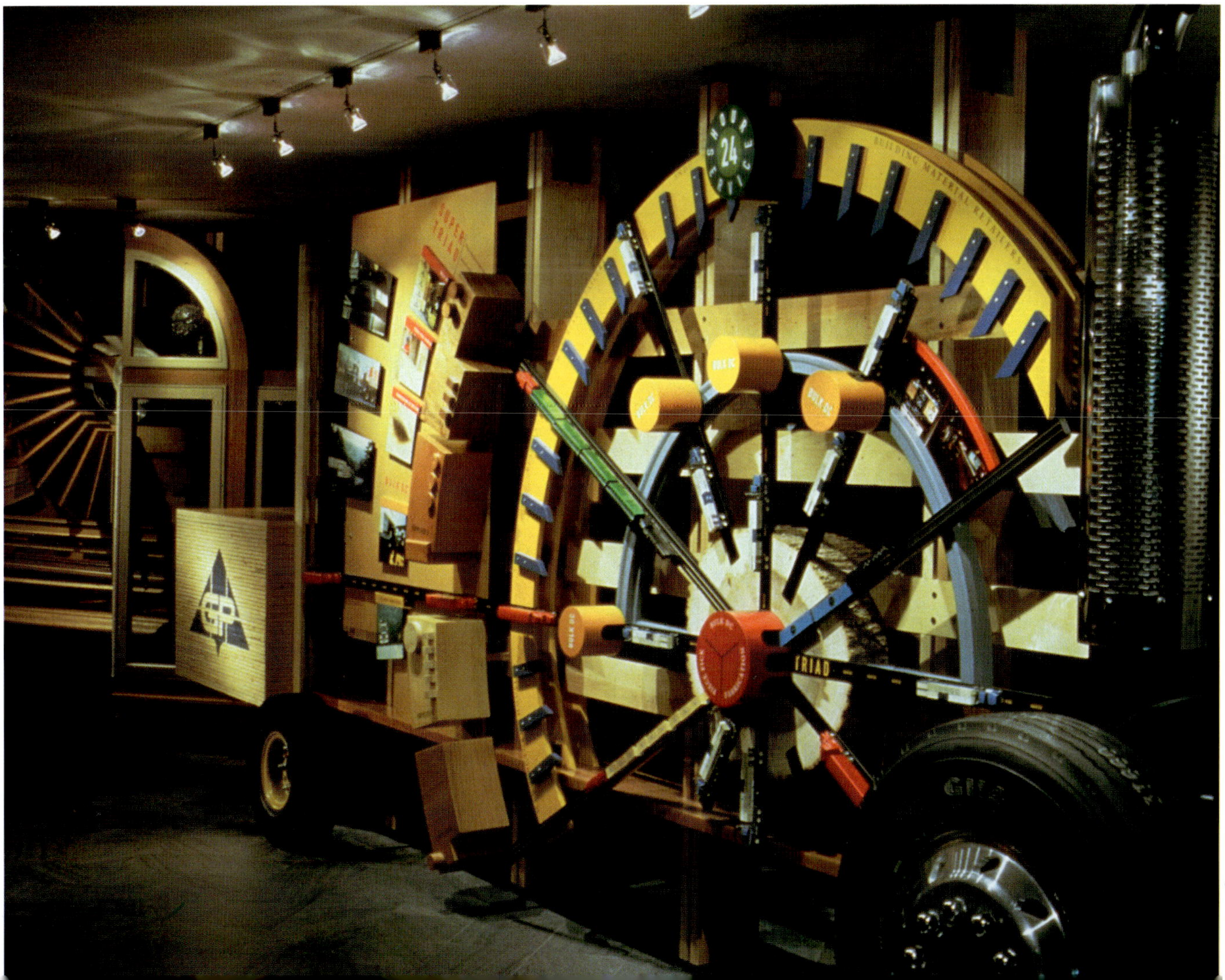
24
BUILDING MATERIAL RETAILERS
TRIAD

DINOSAUR MYSTERIES

15,000 SQUARE FEET

Maryland Science Center, Baltimore, MD
Design: *Patrick Rogan*
Fabrication: *Explus*
Globe Technical Design: *Explus and Moss, Inc.*
Globe Fabrication: *Moss, Inc.*
Photography: *Neil Greentree*

The focal element—other than the dinosaurs—in the Dinosaur Mysteries exhibit in the Maryland Science Center is the 24 ft. diameter translucent globe that hangs in the center of the 15,000 sq. ft. space. It is a dynamic graphic that shows the layers of life and the changes in the planet Earth. The globe, produced by Moss, Inc., is made of printed fabric tension stretched over an aluminum frame and it has a cut out area to reveal a series of layers stacked within.

Unlike most museum dinosaur displays, Dinosaur Mysteries, as designed by Patrick Rogan and fabricated by Explus, is almost all hands-on. Visitors are welcome to touch the full size dinosaurs, pick up artifacts and fossils and even simulate the sounds that dinosaurs may have made. Children are invited to sit in a re-created 7 ft. dinosaur nest and partake of the family-oriented activities embedded in a recreated rock wall with sediment layers.

Large monitors depict Pangea and the continental drift over time while computer stations enable guests to create and color their own dinosaurs. There are also tanks filled with live lizards, salamanders and frogs to introduce the visitor as to how the prehistoric dinosaurs evolved into these current creatures.

This exhibit contains 13 full scale dinosaurs made from fossils and casts of actual specimens recovered in the field. In the field lab area of the exhibit, interactivities include assembling bones and skeletons and "uncovering artifacts" using airscribe tools.

"Dinosaur Mysteries reinforces the message that science is interesting, engaging, thought-provoking, challenging and fun."

HONG KONG JOCKEY CLUB DRUG INFORMATION CENTER

Admiralty, Hong Kong
Design: *Met Design Studios, Hong Kong & London + Kingsmen, Hong Kong*
Fabrication: *Kingsmen, Hong Kong*
Photography: *Courtesy of Kingsmen*

18,000 SQUARE FEET

172

The Hong Kong division of Kingsmen Exhibits was commissioned by the Architectural Services Department to provide the construction management, fabrication and installation of the 18,000 sq. ft. exhibit for the Hong Kong Jockey Club Drug Information Center at The Admiralty. The concept was conceived by MET of Hong Kong & London and Kingsmen who contributed to the technical development of the design.

The bi-level exhibit, as produced, made creative use of numerous multimedia display setups and interactive games—all set into "a lively, colorful and comfortable environment." "The underlying aim of the Center was to provide visitors with correct information about drugs and to assist them in making informed decisions when being tempted with drugs."

HONG KONG JOCKEY CLUB DRUG INFORMATION CENTER

The area is brilliant in primary red, yellow and blue colors set off against white. There are numerous graphics used throughout the space that carry through the same bright sand attractive color palette. A series of individual "play" stations, painted blue, are located under the over-hanging mezzanine while in a collection of red caban-as—located up front near the windows where passersby can be attracted—there are sit down spaces furnished with flat plasma screens upon which images and messages are projected. One long illuminated wall consists of many 8 ft. tall graphic panels—in full color—that explain what the exhibit is all about.

This exhibit and the Center will continue to be the focal point for drug prevention activities in Hong Kong. It is the first ever permanent exhibition center dedicated to drug prevention in Hong Kong and also the first of its kind in the Asian Pacific region.

Club Drug InfoCentre
Agent
Environment
Interactive Theatre
Classroom
Thematic Exhibition
Info Café
Library
Host
Toilet

HKJC
DIC